ROUTLEDGE LIBRARY EDITIONS: HIGHER EDUCATION

Volume 30

UNIVERSITIES, EDUCATION AND THE NATIONAL ECONOMY

T0386196

UNIVERSITIES, EDUCATION AND THE NATIONAL ECONOMY

Edited by
MICHAEL D. STEPHENS

Routledge
Taylor & Francis Group

LONDON AND NEW YORK

First published in 1989 by Routledge

This edition first published in 2019
by Routledge
2 Park Square, Milton Park, Abingdon, Oxon OX14 4RN

and by Routledge
52 Vanderbilt Avenue, New York, NY 10017

Routledge is an imprint of the Taylor & Francis Group, an informa business

British Library Cataloguing in Publication Data
A catalogue record for this book is available from the British Library

ISBN: 978-1-138-32388-9 (Set)
ISBN: 978-0-429-43625-3 (Set) (ebk)
ISBN: 978-1-138-62592-1 (Volume 30) (hbk)
ISBN: 978-1-138-31073-5 (Volume 30) (pbk)
ISBN: 978-0-429-45926-9 (Volume 30) (ebk)

Publisher's Note
The publisher has gone to great lengths to ensure the quality of this reprint but points out that some imperfections in the original copies may be apparent.

Disclaimer
The publisher has made every effort to trace copyright holders and would welcome correspondence from those they have been unable to trace.

Universities, Education and the National Economy

Edited by
MICHAEL D. STEPHENS

ROUTLEDGE
London and New York

First published 1989
by Routledge
11 New Fetter Lane, London EC4P 4EE
29 West 35th Street, New York, NY 10001

Typeset by LaserScript Ltd, Mitcham, Surrey
Printed and bound in Great Britain by
Biddles Ltd, Guildford and King's Lynn

British Library Cataloguing in Publication Data

Universities, education and the national economy.
   1. Great Britain. Universities. Relations with industries
   I. Stephens, Michael D. (Michael Dawson), 1936-
378'.103

   ISBN 0-415-01951-6

Library of Congress Cataloging in Publication Data

Universities, education, and the national economy.
   Includes index.
   1. Education, Higher–Economic aspects. 2. Higher
education and state. I. Stephens, Michael Dawson.
LC67.6.U55   1989   338.4'7378   88-32293
   ISBN 0-415-01951-6

Contents

For Dr Caroline Stephens

Contributors

SIR ALAN H. COOK

Professor Sir Alan Cook, FRS, has been the University of Cambridge's Jacksonian Professor of Natural Philosophy since 1972, and Master of Selwyn College since 1983. He was educated at Westcliff High School for Boys and Corpus Christi College, Cambridge (MA, PhD, ScD). He was a research student, then Research Assistant, Department of Geodesy and Geophysics, Cambridge (1946–51); Metrology Division, National Physical Laboratory, Teddington, 1952; Visiting Fellow, Joint Institute for Laboratory Astrophysics, Boulder, Colorado, 1965–6; Superintendent, Standards (subsequently Quantum Metrology) Division, National Physical Laboratory, 1966–9; Professor of Geophysics, University of Edinburgh, 1969–72; Cambridge University, Fellow, King's College, 1972–83; Head of Department of Physics, 1979–84; Visiting Professor in the University of California, 1981–2. His publications include *Gravity and the Earth* (1969), *Global Geophysics* (1970), *Interference of Electromagnetic Waves* (1971), *Physics of the Earth and Planets* (1973), *Celestial Masers* (1977), *Interiors of the Planets* (1980), *The Motion of the Moon* (1988).

REX COUPLAND

Professor R.E. Coupland graduated in medicine from the University of Leeds in 1947. After hospital appointments in Leeds General Infirmary and the RAF he embarked upon a career in medical science and anatomy, working in Leeds University and the University of Minnesota, until 1958, when he was appointed Cox Professor of Anatomy, Queen's College, Dundee, University of St Andrews. Research interests have concerned aspects of neuroendocrinology and in particular the structure, function and control of catecholamine secreting tissues – especially chromaffin cells – and their clinical relevance. For the past fifteen years he has also been concerned with the development and clinical application of magnetic resonance imaging. Throughout his career he has worked closely with clinicians and clinical units. In 1967 he was invited to participate in the founding of the first new medical school of the twentieth century, in Nottingham, and became involved in the physical planning of the school and its curriculum in anticipation of the admission of the first students in 1970. Since that time he has participated in the activities of the Medical School, University of Nottingham, and health authorities. He was appointed Honorary Regional Hospital Board Consultant in 1970 and has served on the Derbyshire Area Health Authority (1978–81) and Trent Regional Health Authority since 1981. Having previously served for six years on the Biological Research Board of the Medical Research Council he has been Chairman of the MRC Non-ionizing Radiation Committee since 1970. From 1981 to 1987 he served as Dean of Medicine, University of Nottingham, and has been a member of the General Medical Council since 1981, with service on the Education, Finance and Professional Conduct Committees. Since 1984 he has been a member of the Medical Sub-committee of the UGC and the Academic Forum of the Chief Medical Officer, DHSS. His publications relate to neuroendocrine research, magnetic resonance imaging and medical education and have appeared in international journals and books.

LAURENCE W. MARTIN

Vice-Chancellor, University of Newcastle upon Tyne, graduate of Christ's College, Cambridge, and of Yale University; Honorary Professor, University College of Wales; Fellow, King's College, London; Director of the European-American Institute for Security Research and of the European Strategy Group. Formerly Professor of War Studies, King's College, London. He studied and taught in the United States, 1950–64; BBC Reith Lecturer, 1981; author of *The Anglo-American Tradition in Foreign Affairs* with Arnold Wolfers, Yale University Press (1956), *The Sea in Modern Strategy*, Chatto & Windus/Praeger (1966), *The Two-edged Sword: Armed Force in the Modern World*, Weidenfeld/Norton (1982).

CHRISTINE H. SHINN

Dr Christine Shinn graduated in English from the University of Reading before embarking in 1969 on a career in administration. After several years of polytechnic experience she took a year out to gain a management qualification and in 1973 joined the University of Nottingham, where she is a Senior Assistant Registrar. Her higher degrees and research interests are in the areas of university development, management, and funding.

GEOFFREY D. SIMS

Professor Sims has been Vice-Chancellor of the University of Sheffield since 1974. His BSc, MSc and PhD are from the University of London; he was also awarded the honorary degrees of DSC by the University of Southampton and LLD by the University of Dundee. From 1948 to 1954 he was a research physicist with GEC. He was a Senior Scientific Officer at UKAEA Harwell from 1954 to 1956, when he went as lecturer to the Department of Electrical Engineering at University College, London. In 1963 he was appointed Professor and Head of the Department of Physics at the University of Southampton, where he was later to be Dean and also Senior Deputy Vice-Chancellor. He was elected to the Fellowship of Engineering in 1980. He has been a frequent author in the fields of engineering and of education.

MICHAEL D. STEPHENS

Michael Stephens has been Robert Peers Professor of Adult Education at the University of Nottingham since 1974. He received his PhD from the

University of Edinburgh. He has written frequently on the education of adults, and on the role of modern universities. He has been Research Fellow at the Johns Hopkins University, Prestige Fellow to the New Zealand Universities, Visiting Scholar at Harvard, Japan Society for the Promotion of Science Fellow at Kyoto University, and Visiting Fellow at Yale.

WILLIAM TAYLOR

Professor William Taylor, CBE, has been Vice-Chancellor of Hull University since 1985. He originally graduated from LSE, and after teaching and lecturing posts in secondary schools, adult education and teacher training, became Professor of Education at Bristol in 1966. From 1973 to 1983 he was Director of the University of London Institute of Education. His books include *The Secondary Modern School* (1963), *Society and the Education of Teachers* (1969), *Heading for Change* (1970), *Research and Reform in Teacher Education* (1978), *Metaphors of Education* (ed.) (1984) and *Universities under Scrutiny* (1987). Professor Taylor is Chairman of the Council for the Accreditation of Teacher Education and of the National Foundation for Educational Research.

Preface

There is a certain irony in reporting that the eminent industrialist who so enthusiastically volunteered to contribute a chapter to this volume in the end failed to deliver the goods. His aide, pestered by telephone and letter, wrote after two years 'your secretary and I agreed that it would be better that we did not continue stringing you out and thereby hold up your publication date even further and that, therefore, the chapter would be abandoned'. I am deeply grateful to the over-worked academics who provided the following chapters with such good grace and efficiency. I think I may have learnt some sort of lesson. Perhaps others need to be less doctrinaire in their judgements. A footnote: the Conservative politician also did not provide his promised manuscript.

M.D.S.

Part One

Setting the Scene

1

Whose University?

Christine Shinn

The thirst for knowledge is one of the 'primal appetites of man'.[1] That thirst was slaked for thousands of years before society formalized learning and enquiry into the *studium generale* which heralded the birth of the medieval university. The Platonic and Aristotelian concept of learning was the predisposition of the self to what was good and by that means to the service of the State. The Christian overlay modified that concept in order to organize educational resources 'to ensure the maintenance of a literate priesthood'.[2]

The Church needed clergy as much as the middle and lower classes needed an outlet for their spirit of enquiry, and by 1300 guilds of masters and students were well established in cities such as Paris and Bologna. Such guilds attracted recruits from a wide geographical area using Latin as the *lingua franca*. These were cosmopolitan associations, semi-autonomous in that they regulated their own affairs and, by doing so, frequently came into conflict with the locality which housed them. The 'battles' in Oxford in the early thirteenth century, resulting in the injury and death of scholars and townspeople, were an indication of such frictions. The acquisition of authority by the protection of Pope or Emperor and the conferring of privileges on the *studia* guaranteed their existence but threatened their essential identity. If the twelfth-century student had been as a pilgrim travelling unencumbered in quest of the Holy Grail of knowledge, then his fourteenth-century successor at Naples, or Treviso, Toulouse, Avignon, Grenoble, or Cambridge, was in danger of losing that apostolic poverty to become part of an institution with statutes and bills and codified privileges and the ambiguous advantages of patronage.

While the embryonic universities had remained outside society their poverty had afforded a kind of strength. Without physical possessions they could migrate if the environment in which scholars and masters settled became uncongenial or demanding. They were not accountable to the communities among whom they lived and indeed tended at best to ignore those communities and at worst to antagonize them. As the universities expanded in numbers and in their organization they became more noticeable and society gradually developed an interest in them. In Bologna the citizens endowed two permanent chairs, as a result of which they had some rights in the selection of the chairholders, although the students had previously held this responsibility. Both Church and Empire understood that they were dependent on education to provide men of learning to form 'an aristocracy of labour in medieval society. They were the opinion makers [who] influenced the political argument and shaped ecclesiastical policy'.[3]

As the medieval world emerged from the thrall of Pope and Emperor and recognized the power of nationalism the universities responded by seeking the protection and munificence of the monarch and his court, and their international nature diminished. The emergent universities were not narrowly vocational in what they studied, in spite of their concentration on theology, but it was through their education that Church and State were provided with office-holders. Their graduates were able to use the Church in pursuance of a civil career, and in fact ecclesiastics held every high office in the State until 1340, when Edward III appointed a layman as Chancellor of the Exchequer. Graduates with a foundation in the seven liberal arts and trained in dialectic and disputation could find careers administering the affairs of the large lay and ecclesiastical households and in the expanding diplomatic service. The Church continued to produce some of the foremost intellectuals of the period as well as some of the most prejudiced bigots, and the presence of the powerful Dominican and Franciscan orders both enriched academic life and impaired academic freedom. They professed the value of knowledge but could not sanction discovery that led away from dogma. John Wyclif was expelled from Oxford by a union of bishops and monarch in the mid-fourteenth century, and there followed a period of limited intellectual achievement at the two English universities before the new wave of humanism followed about a century later.

By the beginning of the sixteenth century Oxford and Cambridge Universities had acquired approximately twenty-five endowed colleges and were, by patronage and benefaction, established as

4

part of society. They had produced pre-eminent theologians, and civil lawyers, as well as men of culture and inventiveness. They had engendered a heady intellectual ardour. Oxford and Cambridge in the 1500s had been adopted by society and had begun to enjoy the stability and material advantage which that ensured. Rashdall wrote the epitaph of the medieval university:

> The power of embodying its ideals in institutions was the particular genius of the medieval mind, as its most conspicuous defect lay in the corresponding tendency to materialise them.[4]

A new era was beginning in which for several hundred years Church and State were so divided that citizens in England could not bear allegiance simultaneously to Pope and monarch. The universities as producers of the trained intellect were seen by both sides as necessary supporters or dangerous enemies and were consequently bribed and threatened alternatively. The universities prepared men for the pulpit, and the pulpit in the sixteenth century was as powerful as the twentieth-century mass media. Between 1509 and 1603 the universities were required to adapt to the beliefs and doctrines of the Crown while it attacked and then sought to reform the Church, created a new Church, returned to the old Church and finally attempted to weld Church and State together in the Crown. However much they professed their delight in learning and however great their bounty to the universities, neither monarch nor statesman would grant the universities the most cherished gift of independence and unfettered development. All of them and their chief Ministers 'sought to bind the Universities in Statutes, to exclude all save those who held the views on religion approved at the time, and often only for the time'.[5]

The universities lost freedom over the selection of students, curricular matters and, most important, the appointment and dismissal of staff and the promulgation of ideas. These have always been the areas regarded as quintessential in the existence of the true university and identified as such in the twentieth-century debates on university autonomy joined by such commentators as Ashby and Hetherington. The pressure on the universities, then, was not to meet a particular demand for manpower but to buttress the existing system by overtly proclaiming loyalty to the hierarchy and by ceasing to teach and study those areas which might create dissent. The monarch's anxiety, implemented by injunction and visitation, that the universities should conform, indicated the power that was believed to be invested in the universities. The State could not afford to allow them to deviate. They were no longer outside society but an integral part of it. The patron who had assisted their development was claiming his dues.

The situation was not confined to England, for it had also affected the universities on the Continent:

> under the territorial confessional states, the last remnants of corporate autonomy disappeared, and the long process by which the secular state had been encroaching upon the university reached its climax. The same formula which had been used to bring peace at Augsburg was the effective formula governing intellectual life – cuius regio, euius universitas.[6]

When relative peace had been restored and the chronicles of burning, intimidation and destruction had ended, the universities could not return to their previous position 'outside' society. Monarch and statesman had learned how universities could be handled. Queen Elizabeth instigated constitutional changes which transferred authority from the body of resident teachers to the heads of the colleges because 'the monarch found the colleges more easy to manage than the university as a whole'.[7]

As the danger to the stability of the State became less acute the restrictions on the universities were reduced but the ultimate sanction of the Test Acts remained until 1871, barring an English university education and an academic career to all those who were not prepared to swear allegiance to the State Church. For over 350 years the universities were first battered by political and religious pressures and then smothered by the complacency of monopoly. Their obedience was required in a period of turmoil when free speech was dangerous but, later, their silence and inertia were secured by comfort. As a generalization – and of course there were examples of men of integrity and brilliance and developments of value – the two universities in the eighteenth century expressed a lack of concern for and a lack of interest in society which set them apart from it. A university experience became a selfish indulgence which men of money could procure for pleasure and which could seldom be regarded as education, since it little changed their perspective on life. The curricula did not reflect the needs of society, not as the result of a conscious decision to contribute better to society by disinterest but rather as a consequence of an apathy and arrogance which reflected uninterest.

This withdrawal from the community in which they were based was the more obvious as the intellectual energy of that community expanded and diversified. The Royal Society was founded in 1662, and flourished, as did numerous other societies which sprang up for the encouragement of the arts and sciences. The spontaneous popular movement which had given birth to the medieval *studia* was now regenerated in the middle-class interest in learning. Bacon and Boyle edited their works; Lord Lonsdale gave public lectures, as did Demainbray, Martin, Ferguson, and Higgins. All these were dedicated to the growing interest in and knowledge of the sciences. Henry Cavendish opened his houses and facilities to fellow researchers. The Society of Civil Engineers was established in the 1770s and within eight years of its foundation the Society for the Encouragement of Arts, Manufactures and Commerce in Great Britain had attracted over 2,500 members. The plastic arts were not forgotten, with the foundation of the Royal Academy in 1768. Doctors were trained either at non-English universities or by apothecaries, and this latter group was also responsible for the support of much scientific research. If the universities would not contribute to society, then other institutions would take the initiative. The Dissenting academies were established to provide not only for the Nonconformist but also for those who saw the need of a more appropriate and realistic education than could be offered at that time by either Oxford or Cambridge. The leading citizens of the modern industrial society were being educated either out of the country or in those young academies which, to the shame of the two ancient universities, provided a better *studium generale* than either of them.[8] Peace, prosperity and power were the hallmarks of England at this period, reflected in free trade, free enterprise and free markets. This *laissez-faire* doctrine was extended to the universities and little was sought of them, as little was given by them.

In the nineteenth century society had to demand the education it needed. With the rise in the dignity of the citizen and the importance of the working class, with increased awareness of social liberalism, which came to be seen as 'liberal socialism',[9] with the recognition of the rights of the individual, first to vote and then to develop his potential through education, came the interest in the reform of the condition of Oxford and Cambridge, the establishment of London and Durham Universities, and finally the civic university movement which created the shape of higher education provision in England until the Robbins expansion of the mid-1960s.

The aspirant universities and university colleges were not the creation of the State. They were instead a response to the needs of a successful commercial and manufacturing society and of communities hungry for enlightenment and intellectual progress. Their objectives were facilitated by individual benefactions or local patriotism. Building upon the extended franchise, improved school provision and the efforts of, *inter alia*, the Chartists, the Christian Scientists, the Parliamentary Labour Party, the Fabians, the Mechanics' Institutes, the Artisans' Libraries, the People's Colleges, the Co-operative Societies, the Workers' Educational Association, and the University Extension Movement, centres of learning evolved at eleven locations between 1850 and 1892. Southampton, Manchester, Exeter, Newcastle, Leeds, Bristol, Birmingham, Sheffield, Nottingham, Liverpool, and Reading all possessed a university college by the end of the century.[10] They were, in part, to respond to the demand for trained and educated manpower for industries based locally, such as metallurgy, textile technology, marine and electric power engineering, pharmacy, and agriculture.

This movement was not an example of centralized national planning. It was not State-initiated. The freedom from political or religious oppression of these institutions reflected their accommodation within society yet isolation from the State. Their lack of ability to develop to meet their potential, their *ad hoc* growth, resulting in duplication or omission, and, above all, their uncertainty of survival and financial vulnerability were consequences of this isolation. Reluctantly and hesitantly the State, by its first tiny grant to universities and university colleges in 1889, took up these institutions whose birth it had not planned, and committed itself to rearing them. University education was thus proclaimed as, in part, the responsibility of the State. The history of the century from 1889 to the report of the Croham Committee is the history of the State and the universities identifying, agreeing, and reshaping their roles *vis-à-vis* one another. Since the function of neither the State nor the universities is static, and since the perception of citizens, taxpayers and scholars is dynamic, the relationship between the two is subject to constant negotiation. A modern complex industrial society has vocational and manpower needs. A sophisticated system of higher education developed within a liberal environment committed to freedom of expression also has needs if it is to fulfil successfully the objectives to which it is dedicated in its charters. The arguments for the rights of the

8

university are interesting, if somewhat academic, in a period of economic growth. These same arguments are critical in a period of recession and consequent reduction in public spending.

The debate began with the beginning of State support. This support from the taxpayer, through the politicians, was not provided entirely out of altruism, for it was recognized at an early stage that the country's prosperity depended in some part on an educated labour force. As early as 1887 Sir John Lubbock, advocating financial support for the institutions, stated:

> The claims of these colleges were not based alone on their service to learning and study; they were calculated to contribute largely to the material prosperity of the country – our ignorance costs us very much more than our education.[11]

The civic university movement in England was one in which the regions, the philanthropists, the enlightened pioneers, and the institutions could take pride. In general men of vision, enthusiasm, and dedication worked to develop individual colleges for the benefit of the citizens and of the locality, contriving that the needs of the industrialist and the aspirations of those registering for courses might be accommodated together within an institution of post-school education.

Southampton's development was an example of the varying views that had to be synthesized. In 1850 Henry Robinson Hartley bequeathed £102,000 to be devoted to certain educational objects. The will was ambiguous. One faction believed that it was Hartley's intention to establish a place of learning and the other that it had been his wish to provide a library and other amenities for the elevation and enjoyment of the citizens of Southampton.

> Unfortunately the terms of the Will, covering as they did a wide range of interests, both instructional and recreative, were sufficiently vague to give rise to dispute as to the way in which the testator's intentions should be made effective. The trustees were instructed to use the bequest to promote 'the study and advancement of the sciences of natural history, astronomy, antiquities, classical and oriental literature, and also to form a public library, botanic garden, observatory and collection of objects in connection with the above sciences.[12]

While the debate between general cultural facilities and the advancement of formalized education dragged on little was achieved save the reduction of the original generous donation. Indeed, it was one of the Southampton administrators who in 1885 initiated a national move by the colleges to secure government financial support for their institutions. [13]

The desire for centralized assistance was made more acute by the precarious financial position of the young university colleges, existing on donations, local support and minimal fee income. Manchester, Birmingham and Reading were all in difficulty by the end of the nineteenth century. By 1884 Sheffield was in dire straits and the Yorkshire College at Leeds was facing an annual deficit on recurrent expenditure of at least £1,150. [14] The government bowed to growing pressure and in 1889 allocated £15,000 for distribution among eleven institutions. The Treasury minute made it clear that the grant was to be of a pump-priming nature 'for the newer and poorer colleges' [15] and the Treasury memorandum which preceded it provided a more detailed explanation of its rationale. The grant would be allocated in such a way 'as appreciably to strengthen the financial position, especially of the newer and poorer colleges, in the beginning of their struggle for existence, and to stimulate local munificence to renewed and greater efforts'. [16] The grant carried with it the need for some degree of selectivity and accountability, and thus an *ad hoc* committee was established to distribute the money according to agreed criteria which included the quality of the teaching and the scope of the work being undertaken.

The evolution from this *ad hoc* committee to the establishment of the University Grants Committee (UGC) in 1919 is complex in its negotiation and discussion yet simple in its fundamentals. The institutions continually pressed the government for more support. The government recognized the growing importance of the institutions (particularly after the First World War). The government was eventually prepared to allocate increased funding to them but only on the understanding that additional resourcing had to carry with it a more structured set of terms of reference and committee procedures. Neither terms of reference nor procedures would, however, violate the essential character of the universities but would allow unfettered development with minimal control. The UGC gathered information from the universities and disbursed government money to them.

The nature of the relationship in these early years can best be described by two statements made at the significant meeting between a deputation of eminent members and officers from the institutions and the Chancellor of the Exchequer with the President of the Board of Education in 1919 – just prior to the establishment of the UGC. The university representative claimed:

> I plead for assistance for the universities on economic grounds. It is a wise investment. It is seed money that will bring a rich and manifold harvest. The universities should be sustained and developed because they are potential creators of national wealth

and Fisher responded:

> I am convinced – and my conviction has been deepened by the impressive mass of testimony which I have heard today – of the necessity of a very much more liberal assistance from the state to the higher learning in this country. And I am equally convinced, from my long connection with universities, of the great value of preserving university autonomy.[17]

The universities had pressed their contribution to the national good and Fisher had acknowledged not only their worth but their unique constitution.

While the government contributed only a small proportion of university income the gentle and 'gentlemanly' control envisaged by the UGC could be a reality. This does not imply that the UGC did not have a significant effect on the development of the university sector. It did. Its values, its perceptions and its judgements were especially clearly communicated to the emergent university colleges aspiring towards autonomous, chartered status between 1919 and 1946. Chartered institutions too were aware of its sanctions, its counsel and its familiar and consistent presence as mediator and buffer, friend, assessor, and repository of information.

Between the two World Wars, therefore, the country benefited from the growth and expansion of higher education in the universities providing more opportunities for its citizens, more wealth for the nation. The universities, which had begun life as individual initiatives, were slowly wrought into a network, not only by the efforts of the UGC but also by the activities of the Association of University Teachers (AUT) and the Committee of Vice-Chancellors and Principals (CVCP).[18] Throughout this period the paramount role of the UGC was to declare the requirements of the institutions for government money, to affirm the necessity for academic freedom and to balance the pressures of accountability and autonomy to mutual advantage. The considerable achievements of the Committee during this period should not be undervalued. The sensitivity of successive governments to this issue and the awareness of university leaders to its importance also contributed to a period of positive harmony and apparent unity of objectives.

One example of an articulate Principal working within the system was W.M. Childs at Reading. He stated in 1911 that 'government departments are and must be the playthings of politics .... If they (the universities) become pensioners upon the state's bounty, they cannot claim the privilege of independence'.[19] Twelve years later he wrote, 'The co-operation, the patronage of the State is indispensable'.[20] The UGC declaration of 1925 complemented and emphasized this view:

> It has therefore been our constant endeavour, in the administration of the Treasury grants, not to impair the autonomy of the universities or to diminish in any way their sense of responsibility. With this aim we have always recommended, that so far as possible the annual Treasury grants should be given as block grants in aid of a university's general income, and that ... it should ultimately remain with each university itself to decide in what precise way its income, including the Government grant, should be distributed over the field of its activities; for without control of finance there can be no effective control of policy.[21]

Such was the general satisfaction with the system that when reorganization was agreed in 1946 it was the consensus view that:

> the acceptance of Exchequer money through the University Grants Committee tends to be less injurious to academic independence than reliance on municipal contributions or private benefactions ... there seems no reason for supposing that, in this country at any rate, liberality on the part of the Treasury need or would involve any such form of control.[22]

Contemporary national and international commentators also noted that the administrative device of the UGC was as financially perfect as any of the empirical achievements in England.[23]

While much credit, as indicated above, can and should be given to all three parties to the agreement – the government, the Committee and the institutions – it should not be forgotten that the dimensions of the problem were considerably smaller and less complex than they became in the second half of this century. Government was providing less than half the universities' recurrent income, a small (although a growing) proportion of the age cohort attended or expected to attend courses of higher education, the 'planned society' [24] envisaged by Laski had not yet come to pass, and universities held a monopoly of higher education. During the next forty years the responsibility for the UGC would move from the Treasury to the Department of Education and Science, and the UGC constitution would be changed to that of the Universities' Funding Council (UFC); the polytechnics and colleges of higher education would claim and receive a share of higher education provision and resourcing; the Comptroller and Auditor General would be given access to university financial records; the Robbins explosion would be followed by student unrest, graduate unemployment and the consequent undermining of national belief in the value of higher education, both for itself and for its contribution to the gross domestic product. All these factors would combine with a perceived arrogance on the part of the universities and an inability to present themselves to that public which funded an increasing percentage of their activities. All this occurred at a time of recession throughout industrial society and a planned campaign to reduce public expenditure, together with a growing interest in organization and methods, management, information and advanced technology. Value for money, appraisal, effectiveness, efficiency, accountability, quality, and selectivity, the investigation of structures, procedures, standards, and governance were the motivation for Jarratt, Reynolds, Sizer and Croham, and were of themselves laudable objectives.

The nation looked in 1946 at its universities and found they were good. It was therefore decided that more resources should be dedicated to them. The debate, however, on the role of the university had never been resolved. The Platonic ideal that learning was the engendering of a predisposition for the good and the true and that:

An education which only aims at money-making, or at the cultivation of physical strength, or at some kind of cleverness

13

without regard to justice or reason, is vulgar and illiberal, and is not worthy to be called education at all [25]

was, in one sense, the purist approach to education. The same philosopher believed that the resultant strength and goodness should be directed towards society and the State. The educated man had a duty to the community. Gradually it came to be seen that the role of the educated man was not only to act as leaven in society but also to fulfil specific functions for which he was uniquely equipped. The products of the English universities were trained to serve the Church and the State, and when Oxford and Cambridge during one period failed to provide an education which would prepare its graduates for the world in which they were to emerge, the civic universities were established to meet that need. Long after the Benthamite philosophy of utilitarianism had first been debated and the greater good discussed Childs wrote of society's dilemma with regard to its universities. Speaking of the universities, he said, 'Unless they are useful, they lose the world; and unless they are more than useful, they lose their souls'.[26]

The 'world' for the universities then, and increasingly so now, was the financial resource to sustain activity, whether from the State, local support, or private-sector sponsoring. It was the flow of good students and their employment prospects after graduation. It was the regard of the taxpayer, the employer, and the government. Their 'souls' were, and probably are, unidentifiable. Perhaps it is unaccceptable in the present climate that they are immeasurable. The soul has been described, in this context, as academic autonomy expressed through the independence of the curriculum and freedom in the selection of students and staff, buttressed by tenure. Whether 'soul' is a concept that can be defended in a debate on higher education for the twenty-first century is a matter of conjecture. What is definite is that it formed one strand of the debate in this century. The interpretation of 'useful', of being fit for a purpose, begs the prior question of what that purpose might or should be. The definition which aligns usefulness with efficiency, and the further consideration of effectiveness, adds topicality and urgency to the discussion.

Newman defended the tradition of liberal education, believing that a university education should aim:

at raising the intellectual tone of society, at cultivating the public mind, at purifying the national task, at supplying true principles to popular enthusiasm and fixed aims to popular aspirations, at giving enlargement and sobriety to the ideas of the age, at facilitating the exercise of political power, and refining the intercourse of private life.[27]

This was a view of a generation before departments of brewing and mining formed part of chartered English universities, before government money was made available in significant tranches and before the successful outcome of a world war had depended in part on the ability of the universities to research into and manufacture optical glass and magnetos, mustard gas, time fuses and shell gauges. He was also writing before economists of education, such as Bowen, Kendrick, and Denison, had proved to the satisfaction of that generation of politicians that there was a positive correlation between the gross national product and the national level of education and an overall agreement between the index of educational activity and the index of economic activity.

It was partly on the basis of its economic justification that the Robbins Report was accepted by government, for that committee maintained that 'Judged solely by the test of future productivity, a community that neglects education is as imprudent as a community that neglects material accumulation'.[28] The committee would not, however, found its expansionary policies on the economic argument alone but emphasized the role of higher education in enhancing the life of the nation, protecting artistic values, and generally heightening the national level of awareness and sensitivity. This elusive and non-quantifiable objective they defined as 'The transmission of a common culture and common standards of citizenship ... to provide in partnership with the family that background of culture and social habit upon which a healthy society depends'.[29]

There was no doubt, however, that the prestige of the universities, their acceptability to electors and elected alike, increased as their short-term utility became obvious. The war had proved that pure science could generate highly effective applications, and after the war, with the development of more sophisticated manufacture, the need for specialist manpower was apparent. When firms like Tootal, Courtaulds, Metro-Vickers, Boots, and Burroughs Wellcome established research departments in the inter-war years the universities provided the employees with the appropriate education. Interaction was strengthened between the universities and regionally based industry and commerce with such examples as Lord Nuffield and Oxford, Metro-Vickers and Manchester, Liverpool and oceanography, Nottingham and textiles, Reading and agriculture. The demands of society changed as food processing, transport and the mass media required graduates able to contribute to these new areas of employment. The consequence was that courses had to be created or extended in organic chemistry, chemical engineering, aeronautics, industrial psychology, and metallurgy. The universities were responding and adapting in a way that the ancient universities had failed to do in the nineteenth century. Their positive response cemented their position in the community. Research fellowships and chairs began to be funded from industry; industry naturally exhibited some interest in the topics for research or for specialist teaching and there was discussion of 'relevance'.

Childs, Dibelius, and Flexner vigorously warned of the dangers that might threaten universities if they had too high a regard for the immediate employability of their graduates or too keen a care for the short-term demands of the industrialist and, often, the public. Flexner encouraged universities to be cautious in yielding to pressures, to be 'extremely critical of every claimant'. He emphasized that 'practical importance is not a sufficient title to academic recognition' and that 'chemistry made no progress as long as men were concerned immediately to convert base metal into gold; it advanced when, for the time being, it ignored use and practice'.[30] Laski and particularly Leavis added their weight to a view that a university's *raison d'être* was the bringing together of various essential kinds of specialized knowledge and training into effective relationships with informed general intelligence, social concern, and cultivated sensitivity. Such a union would allow the universities to remain 'recognised symbols of cultural tradition'.[31]

The UGC could not stand aside from the debate and did not hesitate to affirm that the universities had a role to play in areas related to industrial need, and should put themselves in a position 'to provide advanced instruction of a specialised kind applicable to the practical needs of mankind'.[32] The UGC was not, however, prepared to support any institution which did not possess at least two Faculties – one in Arts and one in Pure Science – and which could not prove that the courses it offered in engineering could be differentiated from those taught at the local technical college. In order to give yet clearer guidance on this latter issue the Committee established in February 1921 a specialist sub-committee on technology with terms of reference:

To advise as to the proper function of Universities in the provision of education in Applied Science with a view to relieving them from work more properly applicable to other types of institutions: and how far and under what conditions Technical Institutions and Laboratories outside the financial control of the Universities can be utilised for University purposes so as to ensure the utmost economy compatible with efficiency.[33]

The final report was a progressive and imaginative one, discussing shared facilities, the duplication of expensive resources, the interface between previously discrete subject areas, and the relationship between the universities and industry. The report was positive in its view that 'industry demands specialists with the highest scientific qualifications. In proportion as they meet that demand the claim of the Universities on the interest and support of Industry will in the long run be made good'.[34]

The recommendations were too radical and were not formally adopted by the parent committee, although informally many of the ideas were being implemented throughout the 1920s and 1930s – not always, however, without difficulty. The 1935 and 1936 negotiations between the UGC, the University College at Southampton and the local authority Technical College were sensitive areas, touching not only on financial arrangements but also on such critical issues as the role of the local authority, the scope of the Technical College teaching, the development of the University College, and the involvement of the Board of Education. The resolution was a happy one because both the Board of Education and the UGC recognized the importance of technical education and the need for its development in an appropriate forum.

The support of the UGC for the applied sciences and industrial links was emphasized with the appointment of Sir William McCormick, the chairman of the UGC, as chairman of the Department of Scientific and Industrial Research. One example of the benefits of collaborative work was seen at the University of Sheffield, where the Research Institute for Glass had been established with the assistance of groups from two associations of glass manufacturers. Out of a programme intended to assist the glass producers came a Department of Glass Technology, then a diploma and finally a full degree programme. The budget was comprised of student fees, UGC support, local authority grant, DSIR capital injections and regional manufacturers' contributions.

By the 1940s nearly ninety firms subscribed to a Glass Research Delegacy, and the high standard of the academic work of the university department was unchallenged. The historian of that university concluded that 'the establishment of the Glass Department had proved an interesting and profitable experiment in direct collaboration between a university and an industry'.[35]

Throughout the period the UGC did not earmark recurrent grant for a named discipline or direct institutions as to the numbers of students to be accepted into any subject area. It monitored and commented upon student demand, noting the increase in the proportion of arts students in the late 1920s but not initiating any discussion on a planned admission policy. It relied, it claimed, on the normal interaction of the market place to regulate supply and demand. It did, however, continue to give advice, often of a most specific and informative kind.[36]

The last UGC report of the inter-war years showed an increasing proportion of the student body following pure science and medicine (19.1 per cent and 23.1 per cent respectively) and a decreasing proportion in arts-based subjects (46.7 per cent). The report was written at a time of mounting interest in manufacturing technology, at a moment of emergence from the recession and during a period of increasing international tension and anxiety. Against this background the report discusses both industrial reawakening and social responsibility. It offered reaffirmation of the utility of the universities:

> It must be remembered that the effective employment of University graduates is a matter of much moment, not only to the individuals immediately affected but also to the community as a whole, since the appropriate use of talent, must, to a large extent govern the pace of social progress.[37]

It raised the unresolved controversy, 'Are the Universities too preoccupied with the problem of purely professional vocations for their students? Is the emphasis, on the other hand, too academic, too divorced from the practical life of men?' [38]

It gave consistent encouragement for university education to be synonymous with an education for life. The post-war debate between the advocates of a vocational education and education *per se* was conducted against the recognition that advanced technological skills had influenced the outcome of the hostilities and against the equally keen awareness that a more enlightened and liberated society should rise from the flames of the holocaust.

The fundamental question as to the object and purpose of university education had been debated, considered, and frequently made the subject of lucid and emotive writings. [39] The creation of the polytechnics and the debate on their identity and function added another dimension to the enquiry. In the late 1940s the purpose of higher education became a question of interest to a wider audience. It was no longer an issue simply of 'academic' importance but a matter for political debate, since with the restructured UGC and a heightened awareness of the importance of the university to society came an increased amount of State subsidy approaching two-thirds of the universities' recurrent income. This proportion, and indeed the amount, grew still further in the 1950s and 1960s until it became quite obvious that the State was paying the piper. In the 1970s it began to call the tune. In retrospect there was an inevitability about events which led from the expressed need for planned national university development indicated in the AUT report of 1944, through the UGC debate on the advantages of earmarked grants, through the CVCP acceptance of the increased initiatives to be taken by the UGC, through the enquiries of the Select Committee on Estimates and the Public Accounts Committee debates, through the movement of the UGC from the Treasury to the DES, the appointment of the Comptroller and Auditor General, the reduction of the availability of public funds, to the acknowledged desire for greater accountability and centralized control. The tensions between contribution and control, autonomy and accountability, are not new phenomena, as indicated in this chapter. The universities today are facing dilemmas which are not dissimilar in nature to those which confronted the ancient medieval universities. It is the extent of the problem and the sophistication of the society in which they find themselves that are new.

After a period of unprecedented expansion based on the Robbins concept of ability and motivation entitling the citizen to an opportunity of university education, followed by a decade of projections, pain, and planning, where do the universities of the 1990s stand – indeed, what is the role of the university as it faces the end of the twentieth century? The universities are now only a part of the national higher education provision, and their traditional monopoly of research and higher-degree teaching is challenged by the institutions in the public sector. They are claimed by, and claim they are part of, society, are debated by Parliament, encouraged to seek independent funding by government, investigated and monitored, still heavily dependent on the taxpayer, independent yet asserting common standards, competitive yet ready to form consortia as the need arises. The undergraduate population will change from the high proportion of 'home' 18-year-olds coming direct from secondary education with school-leaving qualifications into full-time, uninterrupted, three or four-year first-degree programmes. A response will be made to accommodate mature and part-time, overseas and post-experience students, many with non-standard entry qualifications, many wishing to gain university qualifications through credit accumulation, and a proportion not seeking award-bearing courses but, rather, appropriate modules of continuing education as directed, suggested, or sponsored by the employer. The academic subject areas continue to become increasingly accountable to the professional or quasi-professional bodies with which they work. Schools of architecture, medical faculties, departments of psychology and engineering are accustomed to relating to the requirements of the Royal Institute of British Architects, the General Medical Council, the British Psychological Society and the engineering institutes respectively. Now schools of education recognize the authority of the Council for the Accreditation of Teacher Education. Jarratt looked at efficiency, the UGC looked at selectivity, and the government looks at tenure. Institutions look at their expenditure and reserves, and consider the vulnerability and possible 'rationalization' of small departments, the effectiveness of their science parks, their capacity for mounting short courses in the area of professional, industrial, and commercial updating, and the need to attract non-UGC money to support new developments. They consider their appeal to the overseas market.

All this is labour-intensive, demanding, and unsettling, yet not necessarily the death knell of the universities as we have come to perceive them since the twelfth century. In order to defend the universities there has to be an understanding of what they are, a knowledge of what is fundamental to them and must be protected and what is peripheral, even if traditional, and can be subject to change and flexibility. Community, quality, and autonomy are quintessential, if relative, concepts. Autonomy is evidenced by ultimate control over admissions, examinations, appointment and dismissal of staff, and syllabus content. The universities have never claimed absolute freedom but require a limited academic autonomy. The Jarratt Report noted that 'despite the constitutional autonomy of universities, their freedom of action is significantly limited in practice'.[40]

The traditional defender of that freedom has been the UGC, and the verdict on the performance of the UGC was, until the 1960s, almost unanimously laudatory. The difficulties of the 1970s and 1980s necessarily brought the UGC into areas of controversy and often criticism. It is perhaps too soon for a final judgement to be offered on its performance but there is already informed commentary available on its progress. Some believe the Committee has failed.

> We can test the UGC's actions by asking how well it resisted government policy, and how far it converted the instruction to cut into measures which were wrong in themselves. We should ask whether the processes of implementation were compatible with academic ethics .... It was this kind of UGC support for government policy that justifies attacks on the UGC, such as that made in December 1980 by the AUT president. 'From being the universities' watchdog (a role which Dr Parkes explaintly rejected), Dr Parkes is ready and willing to become the government's hatchet man.' [41]

Others argued that the UGC had had an almost impossible task and that it performed as well as could be expected within the given parameters. The parameters may need to be changed.

> The problem, of course, lies in the definition of national need .... It could be argued that when expansion and resources went hand in hand there was a greater possibility that universities might experiment and diversify, but in fact this did not happen, and the UGC offered no incentives to assist the process .... If the UGC is truly to maintain a university system 'of outstanding quality' (UGC 1984) it needs to broaden its own 'mission'. Academic criteria and the maintenance of academic quality, essential though they are, cannot be the only basis for the management of the system. [42]

The Croham Report in its review of the UGC began by articulating the traditional tension: 'University autonomy and State funding, with responsibility to Parliament, are principles whose co-existence requires compromise.' [43] Although the report reaffirmed the accepted practice of government non-interference in resource distribution, emphasizing that the government 'should give no guidance or direction in this respect' [44] many, among them vice-chancellors, received it with concern and disappointment. During the House of Lords debate on the report Lord Swann anticipated that universities would continue to be 'so laden with administrative chores and so harassed by bureaucrats pursuing dubious performance indicators' [45] that the best of their staff would leave the system. The Vice-Chancellor of Cambridge warned that further centralized control would jeopardize the life of the universities, saying that the main thrust of the report 'is to drive yet another nail into the coffin of autonomy'. [46]

The White Paper which succeeded the report recommended changes to the UGC, including the establishment of a Universities Funding Council (UFC) created to 'clarify responsibilities, improve financial accountability and increase effectiveness'. [47] The Minister for Higher Education explained that the body had been retitled since the term 'grants' was somewhat feudal in interpretation, while 'funding' afforded a more neutral concept. [48] Croham had included in its terms of reference of the UGC the existing role of reviewing the needs of universities and reporting them to government. The White Paper UFC is not to possess such a remit. The UFC will have increased non-academic membership and will allocate funds annually, with indicated allocations for a further two-year period. Neither of these recommendations will increase the confidence of universities for strategic planning purposes.

None of this is to deny a need for change. The universities should not be allowed to petrify in a fossilized system but should be dynamic and open to that 'perpetual modification' [49] advocated by Rashdall. Those modifications can best be initiated or accepted if universities acknowledge that they are a part of contemporary society, and if, while retaining objectivity, that society welcomes and supports them, recognizing that level of achievement and defending those functions proclaimed again after recent analysis and evaluation. Jarratt claimed:

> The UK universities make outstanding contributions to our national life. Their three year degree courses (four year in Scotland) are shorter than those of any other developed country and their wastage rate is low not least because of their emphasis on small group teaching and personal tuition. They play the leading role in maintaining and advancing scholarship in the

humanities and the social sciences, where their achievements are high by international standards. They carry out the greater part of the pure research in the United Kingdom and much of the applied research on which future scientific and technological development depends. In consequence they provide most of the country's pure and applied research workers in science, engineering, medicine and other fields and they underpin in culture and the arts the quality of national life. We support the UGC's view that any policy that diminished the role and status of the universities could damage many aspects of our educational, cultural and industrial life.[50]

The White Paper endorsed these beliefs.

British universities have a proud tradition. It is the responsibility of society to ensure that they have a viable future.

NOTES

1. H.A.L. Fisher, *A History of Europe*, London, 1936, p. 245.

2. A.B. Cobban, *The Medieval Universities: their Development and Organisation*, London, 1975.

3. ibid., p.234.

4. H. Rashdall (ed.), *The Universities of Europe in the Middle Ages*, I, Oxford, 1936, p.3.

5. A. Mansbridge, *The Older Universities of England*, London, 1923, p.55.

6. R. Hofstader and U. Metzger (eds), *The Development of Academic Freedom in the United States*, New York, 1955, p.7. The Augsburg peace was an attempt at compromise between the Catholic and Protestant doctrines.

7. Royal Commission on Oxford and Cambridge Universities (1958), as quoted by R.O. Berdahl, *British Universities and the State*, Berkeley, CA, 1959, p.15.

8. William Hazlitt had been a student at Hackney College and reflected this view.

9. D. Thomson, *England in the Nineteenth Century*, Pelican History of England, VIII, London, 1950, p.193.

10. The dates were: Southampton 1850, Manchester 1851, Exeter 1865, Newcastle 1871, Leeds 1874, Bristol 1876, Birmingham and Sheffield 1880, Nottingham 1881, Liverpool 1882, and Reading 1892.

11. *The Times*, 1 July 1887.

12. Professor G.G. Dudley, Historical note, Collection for the University College, Centenary Celebration, 1950, Special University Collection, University of Southampton.

13. Shore, the executive officer at Southampton, played a key role in the campaign for grant in 1885. The lead soon passed from this small

college, which ironically was excluded from the 1889 grant distribution.

14. P.H.J.H. Gosden and A.J. Taylor (eds), *Studies in the History of a University, 1874–1974*, Leeds, 1975, p. 88.

15. Treasury Minutes, 11 March 1889, UGC Archives, PRO, Kew.

16. ibid.

17. Minutes of the Proceedings of the Deputation (1919), 23 November 1918, p. 35.

18. The Memorandum of Association of the CVCP was registered under the Companies Act as part of the Universities Bureau in July 1919. The title of the AUT was agreed in June 1919, and the first international congress of the NUS was held in Strasbourg in 1919.

19. W.M. Childs, 'The State and the freedom of the English universities', *Edinburgh Review*, January 1911.

20. Id., *Universities and the State*, 1923.

21. University Grants Committee, *Report including Returns from Universities and University Colleges in Receipt of Treasury Grants for the Academic Year 1923–24*, London, 1925, p.13.

22. University Grants Committee, Memorandum on Questions of Principle affecting Post-war Grants to the Universities, London, September 1944, p. 1.

23. This was certainly the view expressed by A.W. Chapman (*The Story of a Modern University*, London, 1955), P.S. Noble (*Redbrick Universities*, 1956), H.V. Wiseman ('Parliament and the UGC', *Public Administration*, XXXIX, 1956) and L.M. Hacker (*Government Assistance to the Universities in Great Britain*, New York, 1952).

24. H.J. Laski, *Reflections on the Revolution of our Times*, London, 1943, p. 163.

25. W.Boyd, *Plato for Today*, London, 1962, p. 149.

26. W.M. Childs, *The Justification of Universities*, Manchester, 1936.

27. J.H. Newman, *The Idea of a University*, London, 1905 edition, p. 153.

28. *Higher Education* (the Robbins Report), Cmnd 2154, London, 1963, para. 621.

29. ibid., para. 28.

30. A. Flexner, *Universities American, English, German*, New York, 1930, pp. 14, 24, 27.

31. F.R. Leavis, *Education and the University*, London, 1943.

32. University Grants Committee, *Returns for Universities and University Colleges in Receipt of Treasury Grants for the Academic Year 1919–20*, London, 1921.

33. Minutes of the UGC meeting, 3 February 1921, UGC Archives, PRO, Kew.

34. Report of the Sub-committee on Technology, appendix to Minutes of the UGC meeting, 9 March 1922, p. 5, UGC Archives, PRO, Kew.

35. A.W. Chapman, *The Story of a Modern University*, London, 1955, p. 273.

36. In the 1920s the UGC warned about the over-supply of chemistry graduates and their consequent difficulties in finding suitable employment.

37. University Grants Committee, *Report for the Period 1929–31 to 1934–35, including Returns from Universities and University Colleges in*

Receipt of Treasury Grants for the Academic Year 1934–35, London, 1936, p.30.

38. ibid., p. 32.

39. In this context the debate between Moberly (once chairman of the UGC) and Oakeshott over Moberly's book *The Crisis in the University* (London, 1949) is to be noted.

40. *Report of the Steering Committee for Efficiency Studies in Universities* (the Jarratt Report), London, 1985, p. 8, paras. 2–4.

41. M. and D. Kogan, *The Attack on Higher Education*, London, 1983, pp. 92, 94.

42. M.L. Shattock, in *Standards and Criteria in Higher Education*, ed. G.C. Moodie, London, 1986, pp. 62–3.

43. *Review of the University Grants Committee* (the Croham Report), Cm. 81, London, 1987, p. 8, para. 2.2.

44. ibid., p. 2, para. 18.

45. 'Lords sceptical of Croham's UGC', *Times Higher Education Supplement*, 27 March 1987.

46. ibid.

47. Government White Paper, *Higher Education: Meeting the Challenge*, Cm. 114, London, 1987, p.v.

48. Speech by the Rt Hon. George Walden to the Conference of University and Polytechnic Administrators, Nottingham, April 1987.

49. Op. cit., p. 461. The whole quotation reads, 'University institutions must undergo perpetual modification in the future as they have undergone perpetual modification in the past'.

50. Jarratt Report, op. cit., n. 40, p. 8, para. 2.1.

2

The Universities

Geoffrey Sims

The subject of universities and the economy is susceptible of two principal interpretations. The one – how the university system has fared as successive changes in national prosperity have conditioned government attitudes to higher education – is very much a preoccupation for today's academics, but is by its nature over-introspective for an essay of this kind. The other – how the universities have contributed to the health of the economy – is, however, not only a much more positive story but one which reveals a remarkable change in university attitudes and preoccupations during the last two decades.

That we did not have historically any system of higher technical education in Britain, comparable to the *grandes écoles* in France or the technical high schools of Germany and other European countries, represents a significant difference in our approach to the education/economy interface, and for this reason it is necessary to begin by looking at the background to higher education in Britain in this century. This discussion needs in turn to look at how we produced our professional manpower for what was a primarily manufacturing-dominated economy and also to the ways in which the universities responded to the need to stimulate research and development. It is at this point therefore that I shall begin.

THE VICTORIAN LEGACY

For much of the nineteenth century England had enjoyed a buoyant manufacturing society, flowering in the Victorian period and based on a pre-eminence in design, quality and the ability to produce world-leading capital goods. By the end of the period, however, competition was beginning to grow in other world markets and there were signs of British uneasiness with the development of mass-production techniques, particularly in America. Britain did not take easily to the idea of mass production, where the role of the craftsman/designer, which had been so crucial in the capital-goods world, was seen to have a diminished place.

The belief persisted that our native powers of innovation were good enough to see us through. True, many of the pioneers of our success had recognized that most enterprise looked better if embellished by a cloak of good education, but the education often had little to do with the creation of the wealth that had paid for it. Among the better-off there was a clear perception of what a 'good education' was, which differed little from that laid down in Dr Arnold's classical principles. For the rest, where education was available it was rooted in simple principles and if you were educated you would 'get on' in life in ways which had been precluded to your parents. By the end of the century, and increasingly in the early years of the twentieth, questioning voices from those who could see what was happening abroad were beginning to be raised, asking whether or not we should be learning lessons from some of our competitors. Most of those voices were not over-critical of what we were doing through the educational system which existed but were rather trying to point to the things which we did *not* do – for example, the German *Technische Hochschulen* or indeed the French *grandes écoles* were providing a professional elite whose education was clearly connected with the development, production and sale of the new goods which an increased understanding of the underlying science and engineering skills was making possible. For the most part pleas by those who recognized the dangers, however eminent their makers, passed almost unnoticed and we entered the twentieth century with a commendable zeal for education for the masses based mainly on the three Rs. Whatever understanding was imparted of the world that we were just beginning to discover, and of its past history, showed little recognition that education in the broad sense had much to do with international economic survival. True, the Mechanics' Institutes had flourished, but then, technical education was a 'rather inferior thing', intended for 'the workers' or for the less intelligent, and, though we did it rather well, a kind of self-generated snobbery left yawning gaps in our ability to address the challenges of the changing world about us.

FIFTY YEARS ON

Despite some enormous strides in the provision of primary and secondary education, to which I have already alluded, in which craft and science skills were well represented, the dependence of our economy on education continued to receive scant attention, and as late as 1956 it was quite clear that 'things were still all right' and it was possible for Sir Anthony Eden to rise in Parliament and state that even in the troubled period through which we were living, 'those with the best system of education will win'. Whilst this was a commendable view there still appeared to be very little questioning of what the best education should comprise, though in many parts of the country the scientific education provided in the newer grammar schools was of a high quality. At the graduate or near graduate level our production of qualified scientists and engineers still remained extraordinarily low, proportionately, compared with that of the United States and Germany. Even more important in practice was the way in which we used them when they finally achieved employment, but this will be elaborated in a later chapter.

It is curious to reflect upon the wartime period 1939–45, for towards the end of it, not least because of the huge diversion of the 18-year-old cohort into the services, the lack of qualified scientists and engineers, essential for needs such as those stemming from the development of high technology for military purposes (not least in the field of radar, which we had pioneered), had put a considerable amount of pressure on the university system to produce people with 'relevant' qualifications. This was exerted both through the direction of manpower by government but also through the provision of suitable bursaries in key shortage fields for those who wished to take them up – but, the war over, it did not yet seem to occur to anyone that the economic struggle ahead could give rise to a need for the continuation of similar measures. Had we ever been challenged we would probably have answered that, provided we continued to prepare for increasing numbers of 'graduates', all would be well. Indeed, at that stage all seemed content to allow the universities to remain 'ivory towers', but the assault on them was soon to come in the harsher economic climate which lay ahead. Perhaps we had never faced the question of what universities were for; and 'more's the pity', for if we had they would have voted neither for the *status quo* nor for the move towards strict utilitarianism which was to plague the decades ahead.

28

This nobility of thinking reached its peak in the production of the Robbins Report in 1963, which laid down that there should be provision for all qualified to benefit from higher education to receive it, in the subject of their choice. Most academics (the author included) would still stand by a modified Robbins principle, for the educational process in this country remains a remarkably short high-quality one, and there is a strong argument for providing a relatively general educational base before specialism or essential market orientation creeps too deeply into the process.

In the post-war period, however, a second curious change had been taking place. Whereas at the end of the war there was extensive provision for pursuing part-time higher education, it was not to continue. Indeed, at the time industry also accepted a remarkable degree of responsibility for putting its employees through the process whilst offering well developed graduate training programmes, especially for its graduate apprentices. Successive economic recessions, however, coupled with the more liberal provision of education at graduate level by the State, resulted in educational budgets in the firms being cut, in many cases virtually to zero, and many of the routes by which employees had hitherto gained their relevant education became impassable. The process was complicated even further by a belief that the reason why able young people were not attracted to engineering, upon which our essential manufacturing base depended, was the low prestige of the profession. This latter perception was certainly correct, when compared with other countries in Europe, but our attempt to raise that prestige by making it impossible for anyone who had not undergone full-time engineering education to qualify as a chartered engineer gave little encouragement to late developers, or to those who had suddenly found enthusiasm for engineering as a result of their experience in employment, many of whom would hitherto have qualified through part-time study. This in turn led to yet another imbalance, for many of those who, at one time, would have proceeded to 'chartered status' through diploma qualifications, having served as technical support staff at the outset of their careers, now no longer followed such courses and the whole structure of industry became top-heavy with an oversupply of often ill-used, ill-qualified graduates attended by a great lack of qualified technician support.

THE 'TECHNOLOGICAL' REVOLUTION

Harold Wilson's well remembered remarks about 'the white heat of the technological revolution' (which led, in the short term, to the establishment of the Ministry of Technology) served as a rallying call to those who believed that engineering should be both more prestigious and better catered for by the universities. Indeed, the establishment of the polytechnics and the increase in status which was accorded to the colleges of advanced technology, as university institutions, in the later 1960s were all part of a well intentioned assault on the problem. There were few, however, who recognized that the context in which 'the engineers' had to operate was changing from one which was product-led, in the sense that any excellent product would find a market, to one which was being market-led in the sense that you could create a market for almost anything which was good or novel. The market, indeed, was all-important, and whilst the engineer still had to accept responsibility for producing good products, they had got to be produced at a price which was competitive and, furthermore, must be reliable and attractive to customers in terms of their performance and ease of use.

With industry still playing little part in the training process there were continual calls for the universities to produce engineers who were cost-conscious, design-conscious – indeed, models of perfection which it was beyond the power of most universities to create. It was quite clear to industry also that, in times of unstable economies and substantial capital movements, there were other categories who were really in short supply, not least those who understood financial control in all its manifold aspects. The demand for accountants and managers therefore grew, with financial incentives so attractive that at the present time 10 per cent of all university graduates finish up in accountancy (20 per cent, in the case of Oxford and Cambridge), and whilst the number of graduates seeking to pursue management courses grows annually, the numbers of those wishing to study science and engineering fails to increase. It remains puzzling why it should be believed that you can continually increase the numbers of those involved in the control and management of a decreasing product base, when the decline is largely attributable to a shortage of engineers who can create products that can stand against those of competitor countries where the encouragement of good engineering has been much more positive.

The problem was not just one of perceived reward on the part of the intending graduate, however. It was almost certainly more positively linked to the ever decreasing number of good science teachers in the schools. The danger was first recognized long ago, and whilst a thorough survey in 1966, conducted under government auspices by Sir Frederick Dainton and his committee, forecast dire consequences if nothing was done, no action was taken by an apparently unconcerned government. In periods of high industrial demand for qualified scientists and engineers, the poor salaries and prospects offered in teaching usually failed to attract the best people, and the shortage has now reached critical dimensions, with fewer and fewer pupils achieving school-leaving qualifications in science of a kind which would predispose them for entry to university on the traditional basis. The experiment of offering university courses for those unqualified in science, which would be longer than the normal three years, has yet to be seriously tried but there are many who would be suspicious of its likely success whilst the reward structure in industry is so heavily biased in favour of those concerned with financial interests. It none the less remains a major task for the years ahead when 'access' to universities will no longer be dominated by those with conventional school A-level qualifications.

WHOSE FAULT WAS IT?

It is fashionable in these times to blame someone else for everything. Governments, trade unions, schools and universities have all come in for their measure of castigation, and so from time to time has industry. But there are many reasons why supply does not always meet demand and, without necessarily seeking to identify one particular villain, there are a number of facts which can be stated.

First, in the 1960s there was little understanding of the importance of the wealth creation process, which could come only from a strong manufacturing base. Indeed, in the climate of those times there were many well intentioned young people who believed that wealth creation was wrong and that the evil of profit-making was such that they themselves could not contemplate taking university courses that had anything to do with it. With the passage of numerous recessions and increasing unemployment these attitudes have changed radically, although there are many, particularly in government, who still believe that they persist.

Second, the problems of teacher shortage will be overcome only when suitable rewards are offered to teachers of adequate calibre in the sciences and the teaching profession can be seen as genuinely attractive in terms of both classroom conditions and financial rewards. Teacher education needs to include a far greater emphasis on 'life after school' in all its manifestations, and this poses some stern challenges too. At the same time school curricula need to give far more attention to the world of work and the sorts of jobs that pupils might do when they leave. Most pupils still leave school in total ignorance of the variety of opportunities open to them as well as of the essential and fundamental role of the world of industry in supporting the superstructure of society.

Third, the universities must continue to foster a consciousness in their students of the other attributes, not least the development of enabling and entrepreneurial skills which need to accompany academic success, if they are to contribute effectively in the world of work. This means not only building on better foundations to be laid in the schools but being prepared to devote far more attention to remedying the defects which are bound to persist in the schools for some time yet as a result of outdated attitudes and inadequate staff. For the universities to remedy this there will need to be a recognition on the part of the government that the continual attrition of university resources only weakens the ability to cope with these problems. Further, an insistence (on purely financial grounds) that most university courses remain at three years in length does not allow the opportunity for people, who will ultimately work in the higher technologies, to be adequately prepared for the sterner demands which will be placed upon them by the rapidly changing industrial structure of the country.

Fourth, it is clear that industry must be prepared to devote very much more effort to ensuring that there is sufficient realism within the universities as to what it is that industry really requires – the bland generalizations and condemnations of the last thirty years have been less than helpful. It has also got to demonstrate that it is flexible and is not for ever wedded to the conventions which have accompanied the 'smokestack' image upon which so much of our earlier success was built. In many of the key industries of the first half of this century there will be no revival, and the past is dead. New products and endeavours will take the place of the rolling mills and shipyards: coal mining will become a high-technology, less manpower-intensive industry, and so on. Once a recognition of the new dynamism is there and full recognition is given to the need for well-qualified, well-educated graduate manpower in both large and small industry, then the attitudes of young people in schools will incline them far more to take their part in what is an exciting, life-creating process rather than in what at the moment they more often perceive as the rituals of the mortuary.

Finally, government for its part, despite often having shown a recognition of what needs to be done, must get over the naïve compulsion that it seems to have acquired during its monetarist philosophy period which expects that someone else will always readily accept that it is *their* responsibility to do it, and *not* that of the government itself. This above all is of critical importance in education, which for so long has been almost entirely State-funded and will largely have to remain so.

RESEARCH

Those who looked mainly to the universities as a source of educated manpower often tended to be critical of the lack of obvious dividends from university research. Likewise the majority of those in universities were inclined to take the view that if research was not their primary *raison d'être* it was, at the very least, absolutely essential as a part of their qualification to teach undergraduates. The argument in support of the latter view has often been misinterpreted, for its justification is to be found not so much in the importance of producing new ideas and discoveries – to be conveyed immediately to the minds of the undergraduates – but rather in its role in keeping alive and fresh, in the mind of the teacher, the questioning attitude which is at the heart of all systematic academic thinking. Indeed, the man who does not do research is unlikely to retain for long the quality of mind that he should be seeking to develop in his students.

During the Robbins period there was plenty of money to enable academics to indulge in the things they felt to be important on the research front, and not too many questions were asked about the value of the expenditure. The research council system which distributed the greater part of the research budget judged applications for grants on the basis of 'peer review', a process through which every research proposal was scrutinized by people of sufficient seniority and judgement to confirm that its quality was high and that the expenditure likely to be incurred was justifiable. The criteria for success were 'timeliness and promise', and this was the basic requirement. Although by the mid-'70s the number of good proposals far outstripped the resources available, academics – apart from those in the humanities, who enjoyed no such comparable provision – were largely able to indulge their interests with little constraint other than that imposed by purely scholarly considerations.

The success or failure of this system can be judged in many ways. It was clear that Britain was taking more than its share of Nobel Prizes in the face of world-wide competition, whilst many significant inventions resulted from university research. On the other hand, in the face of a declining economy, it was argued that research seemed to have added little to the competitiveness of industry, either in the creation of new products or by aiding absorption of new technology. It was in fact this latter argument that prevailed, and slowly, from the '60s onwards, the universities sought more and more to adapt a proportion of their research to what were seen to be the 'needs of industry'.

The Science Research Council, under the stimulus of its then chairman, Sir Brian Flowers, established an Engineering Board which in due course developed a wide range of schemes to sponsor research which *was* thought to be of specific national importance. For the most part there was little central policy as to what *was* of national importance, and governments of all shades went to some pains to stay out of the discussion. None the less the Science and Engineering Research Council, as it later became, had some notable successes. These fell broadly into two classes. There were those schemes primarily intended to supply research of industrial relevance where no such research already existed on an adequate scale, and those which were intended, through research integrated with training, to produce, through induction schemes carried out in collaboration with industry, the kind of manpower which was either in short supply or which was needed for innovative purposes.

Within the first category there were two primary divisions of project. There were those conducted through the setting up of directorates which were jointly sponsored by the SERC and the Department of Trade and Industry, the first two of which, in the fields of polymer engineering and in marine technology, later became privatized. Both involved significant collaboration between universities and industry in defining areas where trained research workers were needed and where the universities had sufficient expertise to help produce them. Other directorates, with different objectives, were to follow. They were accompanied, at the same time, by 'Specially Promoted Projects' (SPPs) paid for from the normal SERC budget, which favoured areas of interest considered to be of special importance at the time – for example, research into the 'applications of computers in mechanical engineering', research into 'medical engineering', into 'high-speed machines', into 'advanced semiconductor technology', and so on. Indeed, so much enthusiasm was generated within the Engineering Board for work of this kind, which was conspicuously nearer the application interface, that many saw the policy as an attack on long-term basic research – by now beginning to show severe signs of underfunding.

Successful though most of these schemes must be deemed, there remained a gap between the research carried out by the universities and its translation into industrial processes or products, and other mechanisms were needed to promote this. The Richards Working Party (September 1975) identified 'the pre-development gap', i.e. that stage of development which needed to be filled in order to convert a research idea into a saleable product. Development work of this kind is now referred to as 'pre-competitive research' but despite efforts on all sides, and notwithstanding the very clear recommendations made by the Richards group, relatively little has been done to improve upon a situation where many good ideas, both for products and for improvements in technology, remain unutilized because the mechanism of effective and efficient technology transfer has yet to be evolved.

EDUCATION FOR INDUSTRY

The other group of initiatives concerned with the induction of new graduates into industry embraced one initiative, the Teaching Company scheme, which was perhaps the most successful of all. The thinking that led to it was probably first crystallized in a report entitled *Total Technology*, produced by the Science Research Council in July 1973. 'Total Technology' was seen to be an approach to engineering which not only involved an understanding of the principles of engineering itself but which also took into account such other factors vital to the economy as the costing, design, and marketing of products. A few courses in Total Technology were run, but with rather mixed results – probably because, however good the intention, it is impossible to 'design-in-anger' without experiencing directly the real pressures which exist only in the genuine industrial context. These can be simulated in universities but nothing can ever substitute for the intensity of the real thing.

The Total Technology idea had, however, been preceded by the first of the serious initiatives aimed at bringing industry and the universities together in the training process. The initial impetus towards partnership was provided by the Bosworth Report, which dated from 1970. 'Bosworth' courses involved spells of graduate training on industrial premises integrated with courses at the universities in specially chosen areas of current or future importance. By 1971 they were in existence in micro-electronics, electrical machines, radar technology, machine tools, and so on. Most of these schemes had to be adjudged to have been successful, although few lasted for very long. The reasons were twofold. The industrialists, who had been so enthusiastic about the concepts at the outset, soon became worried about questions of commercial security, and the idea of students from one firm doing their industrial training on the premises of another was of deep concern to some. It is a peculiarity of the British system that commercial security has always stood in the way of corporate development of industry in a way which is quite unthinkable in many other countries, including the United States. But stand in the way it did, as did the 'pride' of several subsequently 'fallen' industries which foresaw no need of such assistance. The second factor was the 1970–71 recession, which led to an extensive cut-back in what was left of industrial education budgets, and at that stage most of the Bosworth initiatives closed down.

The conceptual foundations had been laid, however, and they were to be replaced in due course by the idea of the 'teaching company', which avoided many of the problems inherent in the Bosworth concept. A 'teaching company' could be created as the result of an agreement between a university (or a polytechnic) and a firm to provide an integrated programme of education and training for its newly recruited employees so that the reality of the industrial atmosphere was there and the problems were also real; as important perhaps as either of these two first considerations, the academics involved would also be drawn into the firm's real problems. There was thus a considerable transfer of ideas between university and industry as well as the development of a new kind of graduate employee who was encouraged to use his engineering principles from the outset in the interests of the products or technological development of his company. The scheme was so successful that within ten years some 200 industrial links of this kind had been formed and the scheme had run out of money. Notwithstanding its success, no further money was found for it for some considerable time, and this is a matter of some sorrow in that there yet remains scope for a considerable expansion. The scheme left many areas untouched, such as that of the small firm, but these will be discussed in further detail in chapter 5.

SOME PARTICULAR INITIATIVES

In passing, one needs to note some of the other developments which were taking place at the time. Recognizing the general shortage of money which was available for research nationally, a number of large companies – for example, ICI with its fellowship scheme; British Petroleum, which established a venture fund to sponsor long-term research; and corporate bodies like the American 'research corporation', which would sponsor work of promise; foundations such as Wolfson, Leverhulme and Nuffield – were all standing by to help in their own various ways by funding research in the universities. This would not necessarily be research tending to help the economy, but it is difficult to generalize. The Wolfson Foundation, for example, ran a series of schemes related to industry, not least one of which sought to identify projects in universities which would increase industrial productivity, and many universities developed facilities which were widely used industrially as a result of the Wolfson initiative. Generally speaking, units developed by grants from Wolfson in due course became self-supporting, and again these are elaborated upon within the context of technology transfer in a later chapter.

Similarly, in medicine, another area where under-funding was abundantly evident, the Wellcome Foundation by 1985 was actually putting more money into university research than the government-financed Medical Research Council set up for that specific purpose. Whilst the bearing of medical research on the economy is perhaps not quite so obviously important as that of manufacturing, it remains significant – for example, in the areas of preventive medicine or patient screening – and Health Service costs could be widely affected in the longer term. Hence few could deny that research in this area was not important to the economy, either in this sense or in terms of the marketable products which could stem from it. In medicine as in engineering, however, commercial secrecy has often stood as a bar to effective collaboration between academic institutions and industry, and we have not been over-successful in getting our act together in this area either.

In conclusion, mention must be made of one further transfer mechanism for university research into industry, the National Research and Development Corporation, founded initially through a government loan in 1948. The task of NRDC was to find suitable industrial partners to carry forward good university research ideas, an enormously difficult task in the climate of the time in which it was initiated. Although NRDC survived as a profitable organization, to be later absorbed as part of the British Technology Group (BTG), it was largely through the good fortune of having one or two outstandingly successful products in its portfolio, though there are some cynics still who wish that those products had not been there and that the whole edifice had collapsed at an early stage. NRDC came into being 'before its time' and often attempts to transfer ideas into industry caused long delays, not least because of wrangles over the patent rights or a lack of suitable adventurous industrial partners. Further, many firms were little better equipped to deal with the 'pre-competitive gap' than were the universities. In its conception, however, there were good ideas for which the ground of today is likely to be much more fertile.

WHERE NEXT?

Notwithstanding our numerous shortcomings, within all this story one can detect many seeds of hope for the future of university/industry collaboration and a more obvious contribution to the economy. At the time of writing, however, something of a cloud hangs over the whole system, since, with the continual financial and other pressures exerted by government on the university system, fewer and fewer universities are likely to be able to indulge in research on the scale necessary to maintain a lead in today's competitive world. The sophistication of the equipment required and its cost have increased substantially, and this has led to the call for more selective funding of research. Thus the preference is for larger 'research departments' at the expense of the 'distributed' research support on which the system has rested for so long. Further, there is still a lack of government belief in the ability of the university system to deliver the kind of results that it wishes to see.

These beliefs have affected both the research councils and the University Grants Committee, whose responsibility has hitherto been that of funding the system as a whole, so that all could undertake research. The resource shortage is now so great that it is allocated only on a differential basis, and indeed the UGC is to be replaced by a new national body whose role will be oriented more to supplying defined need and ensuring 'value for money' rather than more obviously maintaining the classical ideals. This in turn causes considerable apprehension among academic staff, who recognize only too clearly that it has always been impossible to predict where in the system the next good idea is going to spring up. Few object to giving value for money, but research will always involve the casting of bread upon the waters, and evaluation of the effectiveness of the process is as difficult as any determination of the scale upon which it should be done.

Whither the unfunded departments, then – for it is far from true that the greatest inventions have always come from the biggest or best sponsored groups? Where also is the seedcorn for the future to come from? Only time will tell, but at the moment the outlook is seen to be bleak by most, and government is perceived to have little sympathy for traditional long-term research, which it sees as having signally failed either to contribute to the economy or to have stimulated industry sufficiently for it to come to the universities' defence. The universities would echo government's wish to see more research-conscious industry, but it will take time, and we are starting late. Indeed, even the majority of university-based economists, who have done so much to condition the thinking of governments over the years, often in contradictory directions as one year succeeded another, are out of favour.

If I have not had much to say about international comparisons in this chapter it is because they are so difficult to make, for few countries compile their statistics on the basis of common definitions. Whilst it is undoubtedly true to say that a smaller proportion of the 18-year age group proceeds to higher education in Britain than in any other country in the civilized world, the definition of 'higher education' is such that the differences may not be as great between European countries, in terms of those who emerge *successfully* at the end of the process, as is sometimes asserted. That we shall, for demographic reasons, face a shortage of educated and trained manpower in the 1990s without a more innovative approach by all higher education institutions is beyond question, and a solution will be found only if government and higher education institutions can work together in a warmer climate than has existed in this last decade.

In relation to research expenditure it is clear that, of the total government research spending, a disproportionately high sum is devoted to military research as compared with other countries. This not only implies less direct support for the universities and basic civil research generally but, indirectly, it affects industry's own attitude to research and its ability – particularly in the case of the medium and small firms – to interact effectively with university bodies which are often seen as not relevant to their problems. In other cases – as, for example, in Japan – the whole social system and industrial ethos are such that many of their often adumbrated successes will not readily transplant to the infinitely less stereotyped and more variable climate of Europe.

There is scarcely the respect for higher education in Britain which exists in most other European countries, but the reasons are largely historical, and it is doubtful whether this attitude would be justified by any hard test which genuinely sought to relate it to the real stimulus that the universities directly give to the economy. All in all the most important thing is that the system should be producing well honed minds which are flexible, and this it achieves in a manner of which most countries would be genuinely proud. Would that Britain was too!

Part Two

Case Studies

3

Arts and Social Sciences

L.W. Martin

The two main functions of a university are to pursue learning and research at the highest level and to teach the resulting knowledge, properly digested and arranged, to those reaching the final stages of their formal education. Both activities make multiple and interacting contributions to national life. Together they produce both people and ideas that employers find useful. But these people and ideas are not merely of practical use in the economy; they enrich life by extending man's stock of knowledge and his capacity to appreciate it, and through it the whole human environment.

An evaluation of the arts and social sciences at universities reveals many 'uses' in the narrower, economic sense, but the value of these subjects is grossly underestimated if the broader contributions to national life are ignored. A nation ought to value the 'uneconomic' uses of learning, and it would be hard to find a significant society in history that has not done so, though there have been many variations in the ways by which patronage has supported such studies, and equally as many different degrees of achievement.

Even if we confine ourselves to the more demonstrable aspects of 'usefulness' we need to take a broad view. That the arts and social sciences make some contribution to economic well-being is self-evident; modern languages help the export salesman, and artists and dramatists support exports and tourism, though admittedly none of this requires a university. The educated graduates of universities fill many positions in commerce and industry, but also in the civil service, local government, voluntary organizations, and, of course, in the apparatus of education itself. Even if we let ourselves be pinned to the most direct contributions to the production of wealth, we need to be very wary of those who, perhaps in positions of political power over education, tell us what is and will be useful. In a fast-moving technological and service economy the most unlikely disciplines and the most improbable people often turn out to be what is needed.

Nevertheless, having entered a caution against the more conventional measures of economic usefulness, the arts and social sciences turn out to be perhaps surprisingly easily defensible. So far as teaching and students are concerned, these subjects receive a high vote of confidence from their consumers, which must in itself be some justification if society concedes any self-determination to those of its members competent to profit from advanced education. It may be argued with some justification that a number who choose the arts and social sciences do so by drifting from an inadequately numerate or quantitative secondary education into fields they think more congenial and perhaps less demanding than the sciences and technology. If there is such a tendency – and there probably is – it may well be related to the alleged anti-industrial bias in the school system. Properly taught, however, the arts and social sciences are certainly not a soft option, and they are themselves becoming increasingly quantitative and technologically based. Many of the social sciences, such as economics, are, of course, highly quantitative, and even the central arts subjects like English and History make increasing use of computers – as the equipment committees of universities are learning to their cost.

All that said, it is probably true that arts and social sciences can be taught in ways that are less rigorous than the methods that are unavoidable in the natural sciences, and those who would defend the former clearly have a duty to avoid such dangers. In the social sciences a drift in the wrong direction should always be suspected when curricula move towards 'current events' and away from established bodies of literature and methodology open to systematic scrutiny by students, usually after having already been subjected to it for some years by established scholars. Where these guidelines are observed, rigour need not be absent and the subject matter is seen to be not less but more difficult to handle than that of natural or applied science.

Certainly the choice made by students endorses the attractions of the arts and social sciences. In 1984, for instance, some 30,000 graduates, nearly 45 per cent of the total 68,000 produced by British universities, were in arts and social science, as compared to 35 per cent in science and engineering. The economy finds such graduates digestible. By December 1984 only 10.7 per cent of the year's arts and social science graduates were unemployed – in a bad year –

and, if this was more than the idle among engineers, it compared favourably with the life sciences at 13.7 per cent and not badly with physical science at 9.1 per cent. Moreover many of the destinations of arts and social science graduates were presumably 'useful' by any criterion: 25 per cent went into commerce and industry, and this, though a lower proportion of the total than of those from science and engineering, was a greater absolute number.

That this was possible illustrates another index of the utility of arts and social science graduates: the fact that some 40 per cent of employers who recruit from universities do not indicate any specific discipline. By this they testify to a belief that being a university graduate of any kind indicates the possession of useful qualities, one of the most important being 'trainability' in future. That is not to deny that some arts and social science degrees have direct vocational utility. Accountancy and economics offer clear-cut cases. That of languages has already been mentioned, and the example of such countries as France, where cultural diplomacy is a conscious means to further trade and foreign policy, suggests that even the literary approach to languages, still though increasingly less dominant in some universities, can be put to practical use. Other subjects such as philosophy, which translates well into aspects of computing, and geography, where economic, sociological and political studies are related to spatial concepts, also turn out to enable many graduates to bring special skills and perspective to work within the productive economy.

The bulk of social science and certainly of arts graduates seem to recommend themselves to employers, however, not so much for having acquired knowledge as for their 'personal qualities'. If achieving a university degree of any kind testifies to a degree of intelligence and application necessary to secure admission to a course and the doggedness to complete it, there are aspects of the arts and social science degree that can elevate those characteristics further. The arts and social science graduate ought to be articulate and fluent on paper as well; increasingly he ought to have at least a preliminary acquaintance with computing. He or she will almost certainly have been left to his or her own devices more than the science or engineering graduate, and will thereby have become more self-reliant in mustering evidence and drawing conclusions from it. A good arts or social science course requires the student to weigh issues, and issues that are rarely fully amenable to quantification. In this respect the problems are more like those encountered in commercial management than those handled by the physicist or engineer, and it may be that the shift of the economy from manufacturing to services will reinforce this pattern. If it is true that what distinguishes a good university education from mere technical training is that the former provides equipment for a whole career, and not merely the opening stages, then there are grounds for believing this prescription is more readily met by the arts and social sciences than by technology and the natural sciences – always provided, of course, that the former are rigorously taught. This being the case, it is natural and to be welcomed that graduates are entering many careers at a lower level than once thought appropriate, as in banking and the police. There is no career in which an arts or social science degree is wasted, if opportunities to rise to responsibility exist.

Turning to the value of the research component in the universities' work within the arts and social sciences, we can start with the underpinning given to the programmes of teaching just discussed. If these fields provide a valuable education for people destined to take up positions of responsibility, the fields must be kept intellectually alive and responsive to shifts in the curiosity and interests of society. Perhaps we need have no fear that any of the arts and social science disciplines would disappear completely if universities could no longer support them. Part of the strength of such fields of learning is their evident perennial fascination both for specialist scholars and, in vulgarized forms, for multitudes. The ways in which individuals find opportunities for philosophical speculation or historical enquiry change with time, but societies always manifest a fascination and some of their members a compulsion for such intellectual activity. But it makes a great difference, easily sensed by those exposed to it, if institutions like universities can provide a home where concentrations of such activity can develop and flourish, intimately intermingled with the functions of formal teaching. This intermingling is not confined to teaching within the universities, for by their work in the training of teachers for other institutions and schools, and by the subsequent interaction which many if not most of these teachers maintain with universities, a broader intellectual market place exists for exchanging ideas and setting standards.

It would be presumptuous of universities to believe they had a monopoly or were even perhaps paramount in setting standards within the cultural fields represented by arts faculties. The role of the universities is perhaps least with regard to the fine arts. A vast range of practitioners and critics exist elsewhere. There is probably considerable value, however, in having institutions which can foster work and criticism free from the immediate commercial and other pressures on the artist or author whose livelihood comes direct from the market place.

The arts faculties of universities constitute an important vantage point, though far from the only one, from which the intellectual and moral life of the nation can be scrutinized. This, if done well, is a function to be valued even if not in economic terms. It is not, however, devoid of economic utility, even if it is impossible to measure. Whole swathes of economic activity have consequences for society, in such respects as design, effect on the environment, and a general impact on taste, sense of propriety, and well-being. If such matters are not kept in tolerable balance with social preferences, difficult and even dangerous tensions and conflict arise. The arts and social science disciplines are central to the process by which societies set a balance in such matters, and it would be naïve to believe this is not of great consequence for the national economy merely because it is probably impossible to measure the return.

The so-called social sciences, of course, are explicitly directed towards understanding and where possible measuring political, economic, and social processes. Use of the word 'science' in this connection annoys some who have a higher regard for disciplines where generally simpler problems and amenability to repetitive experiment permit more quantification. The tendency of many who study social phenomena to concentrate on 'problems' and to proceed to prescription has also generated considerable political suspicion of the social sciences. Some of it is undoubtedly justified; there is no denying that reformist concern brings many into the social sciences who are more interested – if often, and all the more dangerously, subconsciously – in finding arguments for preconceived programmes than in objective analysis. Nevertheless, no one can dismiss the relevance of sound analysis to the effective management of society and promotion of its welfare.

Economics enjoys especially wide approval for being obviously relevant to the concerns of both 'right' and 'left', but it may be that the fact that its subject matter is the production and distribution of material wealth distracts attention from the relatively limited success of economists in providing politicians with the guidance to achieve reliable results. In reality, all the social sciences deal with immensely complex phenomena and with often inherently intractable problems.

This does not mean, however, that we can dispense with systematic analysis. Critics of the social sciences frequently suggest, particularly in the Anglo-Saxon cultures, that 'common sense' is a better guide. Sometimes pretentious social science merely garbs common sense in jargon; at its worst it may do the same for nonsense. But, at its best, social science lays bare the unspoken and all too often false assumptions and reasoning that pass for common sense. This can be so even for such grand issues as those of war and peace. Stimulated by the challenge of nuclear weapons, for instance, economists and historians led the way toward systematizing theories of deterrence and in developing the concepts of arms control. Doubtless soldiers and statesmen would have groped their way towards such practices even without an articulated theory, but there can be no doubt that a burst of thinking in academic circles, chiefly American and British, in the 1960s crystallized the theoretical nature of this immensely important set of social relations rapidly and explicitly, and accelerated their permeation of the military and diplomatic operation.

In doing so these social scientists were helping to interpret the implications of technological change for society. This is a general and most important function of the social scientist and of those such as historians and philosophers who are not always grouped under that label. Much of the political pressure in Britain today for academics to come to the rescue of the economy – pressure that is in itself some testimony to lack of faith in the economy's capacity to prosper without them – has to do with the development and application of technology. It is increasingly apparent, however, that this is probably much more a social than a technological problem. Whatever its precise merits, the frequently heard complaint that the British are fertile in invention but poor at application and development identifies not a technological but a psychological and social problem. Moreover, this problem is not merely one of how to stimulate people to be effective in the economy but also of what the price of such effectiveness may be and whether citizens really want to pay it.

Unquestionably the most widely touted panacea for economic ills today, the alchemist's stone looked to for success, is 'information technology'. The technology races on apace. What seems difficult is its effective application to generating prosperity in Britain. Part of the difficulty lies in uncertainty as to whether the consequences of information technology are benign or can be made so. There is thus an immense range of problems concerning both the applicability and the tolerability of the new information techniques. Those who tackle these problems will be engaged in social engineering and, whether or not they consciously call the knowledge and techniques of the social scientist to their aid, they will inevitably do so in practice.

It seems much better that they do so consciously, and they will find the greatest repository of knowledge and skill in the universities. Furthermore, in the vast range of approaches to be found in the academic world at large is the best available assurance against the prejudice, preconception, and bias that are undeniably a recurrent hazard in such work.

It is encouraging, therefore, that the Economic and Social Science Research Council has perceived the need and established two or three major programmes of research and teaching – the first two at Newcastle and Sussex – to tackle the social and economic consequence of the so-called information revolution. The unit at Newcastle to which this work has been entrusted, the Centre for Urban and Regional Development Studies (CURDS), offers a specific and encouraging illustration of how systematic analysis at universities can unmask apparently sensible but really mistaken assumptions and bring about a change in national policy.

For many years it has been an assumption of regional development policy that the economic regeneration of the less prosperous areas required, among other things, not merely the direct subsidy of jobs but the encouragement of a local capacity to innovate and to generate intra-regional trade, preferably in relatively high-technology products. A preferred way of doing this was to persuade major national and international companies to set up branch factories in the regions, enticed by subsidies and concessions.

Analysis by CURDS of what was actually happening, however, revealed that branch factories are extremely ineffective in producing these effects. Branch factories typically lack the research arms and the managerial authority to innovate. Moreover they commonly lack the authority to purchase locally on a large scale. Consequently they neither grow dynamically themselves nor spin off ideas to other local business, even by example. Similarly the local networks of trade fail to develop. All these benign phenomena remain for the most part within the ambit of the parent company in the more prosperous regions or even abroad.

These unwelcome findings relatively quickly won a hearing among economic planning authorities both in the United Kingdom and within the European Economic Community (EEC). As a result a considerable change has come over official thinking. The consequences can be seen in the 1983 British Green Paper *Regional Industrial Development* and in the EEC Council Regulation of June 1984 on the European Regional Development Fund, in both of which much more precise and demanding requirements with regard to the likelihood of generating indigenous regional innovation are laid down as conditions for securing aid.

In theory it is not necessary to embed such social research in a university. The fact remains that it was so embedded, and it must be doubted whether such lateral critiques of accepted wisdom could arise so freely within government or commerce itself. Moreover the combination of the functions of research and teaching within a single, multi-disciplinary institution produces not merely a uniquely fertile intellectual environment but a cost-effective one.

That is not to say that the university should be insulated from government or the other sources of social thought and policy. On the contrary, results such as the one just described demand close links between the university social scientists and their political and commercial counterparts. It is a failing of the British system to be less favourable to such links than many other national systems. In particular the frequent interchange of personnel between the universities on the one hand and government and business on the other, fruitful in such countries as the United States, is peculiarly difficult in Britain and should be facilitated. What is often said of the relations between British universities and government can also be said to a large extent of the universities and business. Already the universities permeate the market of ideas that underlies British economic and social policy to a much greater extent than is commonly realized, just as their academic colleagues in the sciences and engineering play an equally unsung part in manufacturing industry.

But in the social sciences and arts, as in technology, the vast resource of the universities is still under-exploited. The fault is on both sides, but there are welcome signs, as, for instance, in the work of the parliamentary committees, that things are improving. The merits of the universities in these fields have long been denied just recognition. If this is to be rectified, the task of the universities must of course be to root out the insubstantial or spurious and to improve the quality of what remains.

4

Education and the Economy

William Taylor

The work of education departments in universities is significant for the economy in two main ways. One is much easier to describe and evaluate than the other.

Primary and secondary school teachers constitute an important proportion of the highly educated work force. Departments of education train nearly all the men and women entering secondary teaching, mainly through one-year courses for the Postgraduate Certificate in Education. They also prepare primary teachers through directly provided PGCE and BEd courses, and help their universities to validate teaching for these awards undertaken by affiliated colleges and institutes of higher education. And at post-experience level they teach for advanced qualifications and higher degrees and offer research opportunities.

Education departments also influence the economy through the values and dispositions concerning children, society, curriculum, pedagogy, and evaluation with which they imbue their pre-service and advanced students. Their staff act as opinion-formers within and beyond the profession by writing books and research reports, serving on committees and commissions, participating in conferences, and broadcasting. It is not easy to analyse and evaluate the nature and extent of such influence, although there are always those ready to sit in judgement upon it.

THE BEGINNINGS

British universities did not become involved in the training of teachers or the study of education in any systematic way until the fourth quarter of the nineteenth century. They took up such work for economic and religious rather than academic reasons. Then, as now, there was concern that teachers insufficient in numbers and inadequate in quality would be bad for industry and for society. In the first decade of the century a contributor to the fourth edition of the *Encyclopaedia Britannica* (1810) had written:

> We will venture to say, that there is no class of men to whom a nation is as much indebted as to those employed in instructing the young; for if it be education that forms the only distinction between the civilised and the savage, much certainly is due to those who devote themselves to the office of instruction. It must be the duty therefore of every State to take care that proper encouragement be given to those who undertake this office. There ought to be such a salary as would render it an object of ambition to men of ability and learning, or at least as would keep the teacher respectable .... But at present the salary of a country schoolmaster, independent of fees for scholars, is not greater than a ploughman can earn, being seldom more than £8 6s 8d. The consequence of which is that this, which is in fact an honourable, because a useful profession, is now sinking into contempt.

Although there had been earlier efforts to interest universities in appointing professors of education (in the 1820s in Scotland, in 1836 at University College, London, in 1873 at Oxford and Cambridge), it was not until 1876 that the first two university chairs were created, at Edinburgh and St Andrews. Scotland also founded non-residential training colleges that offered a model for many of those who looked to the Royal Commission on the Working of the Elementary Education Acts in England and Wales (the Cross Commission) for improvements in the quantity and quality of teacher training. A high proportion of the existing residential training colleges south of the border imposed religious tests. But when it reported in 1888 the Cross Commission was hardly enthusiastic about recommending the setting up of secular day training colleges associated with universities: '... we think it might be well that some such experiments should be made, subject to the condition, that only a limited number of students should receive government assistance towards their training.' The response of the universities, given their financial position, was much less cautious. Government initially set an overall limit of 200 students in such colleges. It was soon forgotten. By 1900 there were nearly 1,400 students in day training colleges, which soon began to assume the form and substance of university departments of education.

In the period up to the First World War the work of these departments shifted towards the preparation of teachers for secondary rather than elementary schools. In 1911 the Board of Education, in the wake of its 1908 *Regulations for the Training of Teachers for Secondary Schools*, recognized such departments as providing a four-year course of training. Three years would be devoted to obtaining a degree in arts or science, the fourth to professional work. In England and Wales, although not in Scotland, where colleges continued to be responsible for the initial training of both elementary and secondary teachers, the work of university education departments soon came to be focused on the one-year postgraduate course that still constitutes a large part of their total activity.

From the beginning, staff appointed to train teachers in universities were also involved in a variety of other scholarly and academic activities. The first two chairs were in the 'Theory, History and Practice of Education'. Lecturers wrote textbooks and monographs, undertook research and gave advice to both official and unofficial educational bodies. The London Day Training College (later to become the University of London Institute of Education) began to offer MA degrees in education before the end of the First World War. By 1932 fifty had been awarded.

The extension of initial teacher training and the provision of opportunities for serving teachers to upgrade their qualifications through universities did little to assuage the anxieties of those who compared our own provision with that of other countries that were already or were likely to become our economic competitors. Such anxieties had to do with the structural and organizational weaknesses of our educational system as a whole, not just the quality of teachers and teaching, although much of the criticism was a spur to universities to play a more active role in the education and training of teachers.

During the inter-war years the work of universities in education developed only slowly. From 1930 they took over some of the responsibilities for examining training college students hitherto exercised directly by the Board of Education. For these purposes, colleges were organized into groups associated with particular universities, an arrangement given statutory form after publication of the wartime report of the McNair Committee, *Teachers and Youth Leaders.*

REORGANIZING THE SYSTEM

During the early 1950s all the existing universities, with the solitary exception of Cambridge, assumed responsibilities, through their Institutes of Education, as Area Training Organizations. The ATOs brought together under a single organizational, curricular and awards umbrella the work of all the training colleges in each region. Initially the university departments of education that had developed from the day training colleges of the 1890s remained separate organizations from the Institutes of Education within the universities. The coming together of institutes and departments into university schools of education was accelerated by the Robbins Committee's 1963 recommendations that a Bachelor of Education degree should be offered to suitable students in the former residential training colleges, now upgraded to colleges of education. With varying degrees of enthusiasm, universities agreed to a fourth year of study beyond the three-year Certificate of Education, taught for the most part by college staff, and leading to the award of an ordinary or honours BEd.

In the early 1970s, with an expansion of higher education numbers in prospect, the colleges of education were encouraged to diversify their work beyond the initial preparation of teachers and to become more fully integrated into the higher education system. The upgrading of public-sector colleges of technology had been responsible for the creation of a number of new universities in the early '60s. From 1965 higher education took an increasingly 'binary' form, with governments imposing a moratorium on further changes of status.

The reorganization and diversification of the colleges of education was greatly affected by belated recognition of the effects that a declining birth rate would have on the demand for teachers, and by financial exigency characteristic of an economy suffering from two oil shocks, inability to compete successfully in many world markets, high annual rates of inflation and the practice of single-interest politics. Between 1973 and 1983 intakes to teacher education were reduced from some 40,000 to less than 16,000.

A few of the colleges of education merged with universities, to create much enlarged Schools of Education. Others joined together to form new multi-site institutes of higher education. Others still lost their identity through merger with polytechnics, with existing colleges of further and higher education – or, in many cases, by outright closure. The separate Training of Teachers Regulations that had conferred a statutory role upon Area Training Organizations were rescinded, and university schools and institutes ceased to exercise ATO functions.

As the shape of things to come became visible during the early '70s, there were anxieties within universities about the future of their work in education. The 1972 report of the James Committee [1] had not been friendly to the university connection. Many of the institutions into which the former colleges of education were reorganized already validated their awards through the Council for National Academic Awards (CNAA). Some universities gave up validation activity altogether. Yet fears of a diminished role for universities in teacher education were not in the event realized.

Initial teacher education numbers in universities did not suffer the sharp reductions that so affected the colleges and polytechnics. The ability of university departments of education to attract graduates with good degrees in arts or sciences to train for work with younger children led to the setting up of several new university-based primary courses. By 1983 there were only fifty-six public-sector institutions still engaged in initial teacher education. But nearly all the twenty-seven universities (in England and Wales) that had been active in such work in 1972 were still providing teacher education programmes.

The need that rapid change in curriculum, pedagogy and methods of assessment created for in-service education and training of an ageing teaching force, recognized and stimulated during the first half of the '70s by the James Report, and in the second half by a greater stress on teaching quality and more interest on the part of teachers in acquiring post-experience qualifications, encouraged universities to broaden the range of specialist diplomas and masters' degrees offered in education.

Systematic curriculum development and, in the latter part of the decade and into the '80s, a new stress on the appraisal of educational outcomes and assessment of performance, increased the research and development resources available to university departments of education and brought into universities many individuals and teams on short-term contracts funded by official bodies and by the foundations.

In some universities, departments of adult and continuing education were linked with departments and institutes to form Faculties of Education. Interest in the 16–19 age group grew, and funds for research and development in this area began to be made

55

available by the Manpower Services Commission. Some universities became involved in training for further education. Official concern for more effective school and college management stimulated university provision of both long and short courses for school and system administrators.

THE CURRENT SCENE

In 1986–7, the most recent year for which public figures are available, there were over 2,500 undergraduate students of education or combinations of education with other subjects in universities in Great Britain. Postgraduates numbered just over 8,500, 4,536 of whom were enrolled for initial teacher training. In addition, there were just under 1,500 part-time undergraduates (constituting 22 per cent of all part-time undergraduates studying in universities) and 6,797 part-time postgraduates (21 per cent of the GB total). Full-time postgraduates engaged in 'academic studies in education' numbered 2,278, and of the part-time postgraduates, 1,361 were undertaking research for higher degrees, as against 3,944 on taught higher degree courses.

Universities also provided continuing education courses in education or combinations of education with other subjects which totalled more than 21 per cent of recorded student hours in all subjects.

All this work was in 1986–7 undertaken by 1,867 staff in education, 110 whom (103 men and 10 women) were professors. In the same year, 1986–7, education departments in British universities expended some £8.3 million from research grants and contracts, £2.2 million being spent by London University alone.

Although some universities ceased to validate BEd and other courses in public-sector colleges during the '70s, thirteen are still involved in such work, with few signs of the once-feared 'CNAA monopoly' of public-sector validation. As a condition of receiving a student quota, five of the smaller public-sector colleges have recently been required by the DES to associate with a multi-faculty higher education institution for the purpose of strengthening their work in subject studies, and in four cases links with universities are involved.

It will be clear that, contrary to the fears of fifteen years ago, universities are playing an increasingly important part in the education and training of teachers, and in many of them, despite financial exigency, work in education is flourishing. Just as in the 1890s financial factors caused university authorities to show greater interest in the guaranteed funded numbers that teacher training courses generated, so today, when many universities are in dire financial straits, the fact that the demand for teachers is not synchronous with the flow of 18-year-olds is valuable in helping to bridge the trough of student demand. At the same time, staff in other subjects increasingly recognize the importance of an adequate supply of well-qualified teachers for primary and secondary schools if later they are to be able to choose among applicants of good quality for undergraduate courses. Hence, despite earlier anxieties about the future of their work, departments of education have preserved and in many cases enhanced their place within their own universities, and collectively increased their contribution to the pre- service and in-service education and training of an important sector of the highly educated work force.

Education is one of the few subjects in universities where numbers are controlled by means of manpower planning. In contrast to other countries, opportunities for professional training for teaching are by and large limited to the demand from the schools, which is principally a demographic function. Central government controls the number of teacher training places provided in colleges and polytechnics, and, with the co-operation of the University Grants Committee and individual universities, in university departments of education as well. It does not, however, control the process of teacher appointment and deployment; that is a matter for local authorities and sometimes even individual schools. So we have half a planning system [2] in which the assumptions made about the proportions of newly qualified and re-entrant teachers to be appointed in a given year depend upon the analysis of historical trends and the willingness of employing authorities to heed centrally provided advice. By the mid-1990s teaching is likely to require a considerably higher proportion of the total output of higher education, compared with the present.

Improvements in pupil/teacher ratios, which would also affect demand, have been steady but undramatic. Money is only part of the reason. There is no clear research evidence linking improved educational outcomes to changes in class size on an affordable scale. One or two pupils less or more appears to make little difference. Quality of teaching is a more important variable. There has thus been a tendency to devote such additional resources as become available to in-service training (INSET), to curriculum development activity, and to better school and classroom management.

The proportion of young people and adults receiving education and training outside the conventional structure of schools, colleges, and universities is now very large. Only in primary and secondary schools is it necessary for teachers to possess a qualification to practise that represents the successful completion of some form of professional training. Lecturers and instructors concerned with young people beyond the age of 16 need no such licence. Training is usually available, and they are encouraged to avail themselves of it, but the basis is essentially voluntary.

National committees have in the past made recommendations for the training of technical college and adult education staff, and concern surfaces from time to time about the variations in instructional competence of university teachers and the importance of adequate staff development policies at college level. The absence of any formal requirement, however, indicates the relatively low priority that has historically attached to the professional education of teachers. It began, after all, as a way of ensuring a sufficient supply of men and women with levels of educational accomplishment adequate for the needs of the burgeoning elementary schools of the nineteenth century. Teacher education is still in many lower-income countries an alternative form of *secondary* education. The requirement that all secondary teachers should, in addition to possessing a university degree or other subject credential, be professionally trained only came much later. Indeed, in England and Wales this requirement became effective only in 1983. Before that date, university graduates in mathematics and science (but not in any other subjects) had been able to seek appointment without any professional training whatsoever. Given the expansion that has taken place in post-school educational provision, and the growth of vocational training, it is probably true to say that professionally trained staff now constitute a smaller proportion of those engaged in any form of teaching or lecturing, at all levels, than was the case thirty years ago.

DISCIPLINE AND PROFESSION

The influence of university schools of education on the economy, however, is not limited by the number of students they register. The research and teaching for which they are responsible exercise a much wider influence on educational policy and practice. The ability to exercise such influence has sometimes been limited by the relatively low esteem that such schools have enjoyed within their own universities. This is not a problem limited to England and Wales. In the words of Vance and Schlechty:

> Prestigious colleges have never viewed graduate study in education with great warmth, in part because of the historical and social forces that shaped the teaching corps .... In a time of tight budgets, high prestige institutions are likely to concentrate their cutbacks on those Schools and departments that bring them least esteem. They will certainly not support Schools or departments that carry a stigma. And as long as teacher education recruits students from among those college entrants who are least able, teacher education will carry a stigma in the academic market place. Thus teacher education will be related to those situations of higher education that need students at least as badly as students need them.[3]

We have to be careful here. Not all prestigious universities have rejected or looked down upon their schools of education. In nearly every country, there are examples of universities in which schools of education have managed to establish a focus upon graduate work and research, and an ability to recruit well-qualified students and staff, that meet the criteria of quality that their institutions seek to uphold.

It has been argued that to choose to develop along these lines entails a rejection of other possibilities, such as closer identification with the problems of the field and the profession.[4] In the United States the graduate school of education has offered a model that all other teacher-preparing institutions have striven to follow, with what are by some considered to be unfortunate consequences for their capacity to achieve improvements in professional practice. Smith sees the university structure as an influence 'impeding the rise of genuine professional Schools of Education'. He contends that previous studies of teacher education in the United States:

> overlooked the university arrangements that throughout the current century stunted development of professional schools of pedagogy. Colleges of Pedagogy have been caught between the restraining influence of the graduate school mentality and the time restraints and academic animosities that come from the fact that pedagogical education is an undergraduate study.[5]

Smith's answer is to make professional preparation for teaching a two-year baccalaureate programme, rigorously focused on professional practice and relegating work in foundations to the post-experience doctoral level.

Whilst there are few in schools of education who would go along with the exclusiveness of the professional aspects of such a two-year programme, there are plenty who concur with the idea of teacher preparation being undertaken on a consecutive, post-arts or science degree basis, and who would like to see the disappearance of the four-year concurrent course. In the words of Hendrik Gideonse, [6] teacher education 'as it is currently practised in the United States – a four-year baccalaureate enterprise – is attempting to accomplish the impossible'. The need for radical solutions is reflected in the proposals of the Carnegie Forum on Education and the Economy, [7] which reported in May 1986, and in the report of the Holmes Group, [8] both of which recommend a stronger professional component to *follow* the successful completion of a coherent undergraduate degree course in arts and sciences.

In England the chief defenders of the concurrent Bachelor of Education programme are to be found in the colleges and polytechnics, where the traditions of the professional undergraduate degree are strongest. Some university teacher educators have recently cast doubt upon the viability of the BEd, especially at a time when the overall numbers coming forward for higher education are falling, and it is easier than in the past to obtain a place on an arts or science course. In common with many in the United States, they urge the case for a two-year PGCE, part of it based on work in schools. But support for the concurrent BEd has not come only, as cynics have suggested, from those who wish to protect their own jobs. Defenders of the degree have argued strongly for the more gradual introduction into the responsibilities of the teacher that a four-year concurrent programme affords, for the possibilities of continuing cross-fertilization between academic and professional studies, for the greater commitment to teaching and a particular style of child-centredness that BEd courses demand, and for the gains that come from studying a wider range of subjects than is possible in a single or two-subject degree programme.

On the other side, proponents of the consecutive degree-plus-PGCE route into teaching point to the quality of the graduates now recruited into university courses in comparison with the poorer average A-level grades of BEd entrants, the higher levels of achievement of such candidates in the largely single-subject honours degrees taken prior to starting professional training, the advantage of initial training being pursued in institutions that also have a strong commitment to advanced work and research, and the preference that many young people show for deferring vocational choice until close to graduation.

It seems rather unlikely that we shall see the disappearance of concurrent courses of initial teacher preparation, or the early introduction of a two-year post-degree training. The cost of providing a five-year course for all teachers will be very high. Governments do not appear to be convinced that the resources required would not be better spent on improved programmes of induction into the profession, more and better INSET, strengthening the research base, or providing more school-focused advice and consultancy services.

During the 1950s and '60s what has come to be called the 'four disciplines' (history, psychology, philosophy, and sociology) approach to the study of education became almost universal, to a considerable extent replacing courses hitherto based on 'great educator' sequences and child study. Although 'four discipline' approaches still remain strong in advanced and post-experience work, they have in recent years been under attack, and not only from outside the walls of academe. Many teacher educators have come to the conclusion that inexperienced students cannot reasonably be expected to make their own syntheses of the distinctive contributions of each of the disciplines, and that courses of initial training are best organized around topics or themes which can be treated in a cross-disciplinary manner.

Even at the level of advanced courses and research, the absence of inter-citation between the disciplines, and the comparative failure of disciplinary specialists to combine their varying talents in the solution of practical problems, have led some to argue that a new initiative is needed.

the problem of humanising knowledge in education manifests itself in making the findings of scholarship available to researchers in other subjects of education. Historians of education have much to teach sociologists of education, and *vice versa*; and both have much to teach scholars of educational administration and *vice versa*. But the easy transmission of scholarly findings across sub-fields requires translation and even the development of some common language and some common concepts. Otherwise, the idea of a problematics of education will remain at best ephemeral.[9]

The claims and status of such cross-disciplinary activity are by no means uncontested. In universities the most significant advances of recent years in some fields have been made by bringing together men and women trained in different specialities. From such efforts have evolved areas of study and application, such as biotechnology, which have gone on to establish their claims to be regarded as 'subjects' alongside those of the existing curriculum. This is no new process; geography is a case in point. But what we are actually doing when we claim to be thinking or working in an interdisciplinary or multidisciplinary way constitutes a difficult problem. Harry Broudy uses a cinematograph metaphor to argue that it may not be a contradiction to insist upon the formal study of *separate* disciplines as the core of a liberal education, whilst at the same time recognizing that the processes of association and interpretation which such an education serves are 'inter-disciplinary'.

> Each discipline may be thought of as a context-building frame, and if genuine inter-disciplinary thinking entails a melding of two or more disciplines into a new frame, where concepts of one are translated into concepts of the other, it may be that we shall have to be satisfied with the rapid and facile alternation of discrete disciplinary contexts. If sufficiently rapid, the alternation will give a fair appearance of continuous motion. The liberally educated mind uses these frames with relevance, discrimination, facility and felicity.[10]

In developing his arguments along these lines, Broudy draws upon the work of Michael Polyani and the English philosopher Michael Oakeshott. Their approach to the development of knowledge, with its stress on 'tacit knowing', the capacity to make judgements, and the importance of example and the master/apprentice relationship in the acquisition of a particular style, constitutes a potentially fruitful approach to understanding what is entailed by a professional education worthy of the name.[11] It offers a holistic approach to understanding and planning professional preparation that stands between, on the one side, the field-based pedagogy of B. Othaniel Smith [12] and, on the other, the daunting task of trying to derive consistent guidance from the mass of discrete studies that have been made of teacher performance and effectiveness.

INNOVATION AND CONTROL

Concern about the quality of teaching in our schools, colleges, and universities, and the effect it may have on the success of the economy, has in recent years been reflected in a number of important initiatives on the part of central government. During the first half of the present century the close curricular prescriptions of the early 'codes' gave way to a more decentralized pattern of control through local education authorities and the 'suggestions' of Her Majesty's inspectors. At secondary level, the university-based examining boards set syllabuses for 16+ and 18+ examinations. In primary schools, the existence of the much-criticized 11+ selection process for entry to different types of secondary school exercised its own constraints on curriculum innovation.

The disappearance of secondary selection, the introduction in the 1960s of the new Certificate of Secondary Education on the same single-subject basis as the post-war General Certificate, and the trend towards greater teacher professionalism, diffused curriculum control in a way that encouraged variety and innovation, at the expense of common standards and expectations.

Although largely teacher-controlled bodies such as the Schools Council did valuable work in promoting more systematic design of teaching programmes within and between subjects (processes in which the staff of university schools of education played a major part), it seems likely that only a minority of teachers and schools were significantly influenced by their efforts. By the mid-'70s, in the face of deteriorating performance on the part of the economy, politicians and professionals were becoming concerned about weaknesses in the schools, not least their effectiveness in fostering positive attitudes towards productivity and industrial success. Reports from Her Majesty's inspectors highlighted serious deficiencies in both learning and teaching at primary, secondary, and post-secondary levels.

The extent to which improved initial training could remedy such weaknesses was obviously limited. The number of newcomers qualifying each year constituted a small proportion of the whole teaching force. The opportunities that an individual has to build upon initial training have much to do with the conditions of his or her first and subsequent jobs, the encouragement and support (or otherwise) received from Head and colleagues, and opportunities for upgrading and broadening knowledge and skills.

But if good initial training was not regarded as a *sufficient* condition for ensuring personal success and improved standards overall, it was surely a *necessary* condition.

Teacher education had long had its critics. It had been argued that insufficient care was taken to ensure that students were adequately motivated and had personalities appropriate to teaching; that courses lacked coherence; that the subject content was not always of a level adequate to higher education, or properly related to subsequent professional roles; that subject and professional studies were not sufficiently geared to the particular needs of schools and pupils of the kind in which students would subsequently work; that teacher education staff did not have appropriate experience for the job; that practical work in schools was not always well timed or organized; that practising teachers were insufficiently involved in the selection of students, or the design of programmes, the teaching of courses, and the assessment of performance.

Her Majesty's Inspectorate initiated surveys of initial teacher education, and prepared position papers on its content and organization. As a result of discussions within the Advisory Committee on the Supply and Education of Teachers (ACSET), proposals were made for the establishment of a national body responsible for reviewing all existing and new courses of teacher preparation, and making recommendations to the Secretary of State for their approval. An official circular [13] was issued, setting out criteria that all initial training courses must satisfy before receiving approval. The report of an HMI inspection of each institution was an essential part of the course review.

HMIs have right of entry to all public-sector colleges and polytechnics, but since the end of the Second World War their position *vis-à-vis* university schools of education has been somewhat unclear. In the early post-war years this was a contentious issue in the establishment of university-based Area Training Organizations, and some senates agreed to exercise such responsibilities only on the understanding that their departments of education would not be subject to HMI inspection.

Under the terms of the new arrangements, which require an HMI report to be taken into consideration before graduates of a particular BEd or PGCE course can be granted qualified teacher status, universities now invite HMIs to visit and report upon their courses. Reports on such visits are not, however, published in the way they are for colleges and polytechnics, this being a matter for each university to determine. Given its central government origins, there was some initial suspicion about Circular 3/84's requirement that students:

> will ... need to have a basic understanding of the type of society in which their pupils are growing up, with its cultural and racial mix, and of the relationship between the adult world and what is taught in schools, in particular, ways in which pupils can be helped to acquire an understanding of the values of a free society and its economic and other foundations.[14]

In practice, however, few courses have failed *on these grounds* to satisfy the Council for the Accreditation of Teacher Education, which has responsibility under the circular for making recommendations to the Secretary of State on course approval, and there is no evidence that the vast majority of university school of education, college, and polytechnic staff are unaware of the importance of a soundly based and successful economy if the political freedom, social harmony, and qualities of aesthetic response that they value are to be maintained.

The effects of demographic downturn on the demand for newly qualified teachers, together with the pace of social and economic change to which the school must respond, have inevitably turned attention to the importance of post-experience education and training, reflected in the new arrangements for the support and control of INSET announced by government in 1986. There are anxieties in university schools of education that, by giving responsibility for the co-ordination and delivery of INSET to local authorities, excessive emphasis will be placed upon system and school needs, and there will be fewer opportunities for teachers to undertake longer award-bearing courses and research. Universities are major providers of both award-bearing and short courses, which are particularly valuable in bringing teachers into face-to-face contact with those most closely concerned with research and development work in science, the technologies, and the arts. The INSET work of universities (in common with that of many of the active subject associations) is an important safeguard against the danger that school curricula will represent watered-down, out-of-date versions of what is happening at the frontiers of knowledge.

CURRICULUM AND VALUES

The objectives of education as a subject, and hence much of its content, have commonly focused on the needs of the individual rather than those of the economy and society. Given that university involvement in the study of education began with initial teacher training, such an individual orientation is unsurprising. Education as a subject was initially a component in pre-service preparation, not a discipline pursued for purposes of scholarship or as a contribution to policy formulation, and this has been an important factor in the way in which its study and teaching have developed. 'Education' has had to be 'educational', not merely the transmission of a technique or focused on the kinds of information used by politicians and policy-makers. Its traditions are liberal rather than doctrinal, concerned with the development of critical professionals rather than compliant public servants. Its utility has been seen as personal rather than institutional, enhancing the knowledge and understanding of individual teachers rather than optimizing the efficiency of systems.

Prominent among the earliest elements of the study of education were the history of educational systems, the ideas of the 'great educators', and the study of child psychology. The stress was on continuity, tradition, and individuality.

There was a conscious effort to lift teachers' eyes above the industrial and commercial realities that were the lot of most pupils and their parents, to elevate teacher education above a mere training in pedagogic 'technik'. The liberal humanism that informed much writing and teaching about education involved distancing both teacher and pupil from everyday conditions and utilitarian needs. In the words of a recent exponent:

> To return to sources is, in large measure, to return to Socrates who lives both at the root of the best traditions in our education system and at the root of the best innovations during the last few years .... The essential dynamics of authentic education always take the student beyond the *status quo* into what is not yet fully known, fully comprehended, fully formalised. Education is quite simply the expression and development of a primary impulse for

truth, a deep epistemic instinct which we inherit as part of our biological nature ...[15]

Recent efforts to reconcile the meanings that 'education' and 'training' respectively have for those who work in our schools and colleges are suspect in the eyes of some because of the freight of class and status assumptions these words now carry. The models that influenced the development of teacher education were elitist and academic, rather than populist and industrial. The architecture and the life styles of the residential training institutions resembled public school and Oxbridge rather than boarding school and technical college. Yet sadly, because endowment and recurrent grants were meagre, the home circumstances of most students humble, the accomplishments of staff modest, and the importance of moral example paramount, the outcome was often petty-bourgeois respectability rather than intellectual excitement.

If we think of education as an intentional, goal-directed, and structured aspect of cultural reproduction, although universal primary and secondary education have extended the influence of the teacher as an agent of such reproduction to the entire population, other influences that reinforce the school or provoke resistance to it are now much more in evidence.

From this broad perspective, many recent initiatives in education on the part of governments can be seen to have been directed towards integrating education more fully with other aspects of cultural transmission consistent with national priorities, prominent among which have been the improvement of industrial productivity, the maintenance of governability, the control of alienation and meaninglessness arising from unemployment, the amelioration of racial and class tensions, and tempering the relative deprivation felt as a consequence of a slowing down of growth, which can affect all sectors of the population.

Many politicians appear to have no great confidence in the ability or even the willingness of teachers to align their practices to contemporary economic and social demands. In particular, they have been sceptical about the influence of teacher education. They would perhaps agree with the American commentator Richard Mitchell, who has no doubt about the importance (in a negative sense) of this aspect of educational provision. He believes that what is done in teacher education 'has had and will always have tremendous consequences', and that the 'educationism' they

67

promulgate is an amalgam of 'post-Wundtian misunderstanding and ... Sunday-school do-goodism ...'.

> From the former it takes its characteristically therapeutic and manipulative methods and devices, and from the latter its pious pretensions as an agent of social harmony and guardian of the public virtue. One way, therefore, it is pseudo-scientific, and in the other, pseudo-religious .... A vexing blend of the illogical and the sentimental. [16]

Nearly twenty years ago, in *Society and the Education of Teachers*, I argued that the dominant value orientations of teacher education during the first six decades of the twentieth century had been those of social and literary romanticism:

> the romantic infrastructure has shown itself as a partial rejection of values associated with conditions of advanced industrialisation; a suspicion of intellect and the intellectual; a lack of interest in political and structural change; a stress upon the intuitive and the intangible, upon spontaneity and creativity; an attempt to find personal autonomy through the arts; a hunger for the satisfaction of inter-personal life within the community and small group, and a flight from rationality. [17]

This was written at a time when there existed in England and Wales some 163 self-standing, single-purpose colleges of education. But, as we have seen, during the decade that followed this entire sector of post-secondary education disappeared. New-style BEd degrees were introduced, usually on a modular basis, with a wide choice of subjects and options (too wide, according to some recent surveys, resulting in an undesirable fragmentation and loss of course coherence).

Many of the staff who had sustained the former college of education traditions retired. Some of those responsible for the new BEd courses did not identify themselves primarily as teacher educators; they were subject staff from other departments of the college or polytechnic. University BEd courses also drew heavily upon the programmes of departments other than Education. Romanticism gave way to some extent to a new instrumentalism, a task- rather than person-centred style that had always been characteristic of the technical colleges from which many of the new institutions had developed. Elements of the former values survived, however, in part because they supported orientations to the teachers' task that remained significant, such as avoidance of so-called 'academicism' when dealing with less able students, a stress upon community, and the teacher's continuing importance as an agent of moral improvement.

Both as profession and as field of study education is culture- and system-bound in a way that, for example, biotechnology or particle physics is not. Among professional fields, the technologies of education are less firmly dependent on basic science research traditions than those, for example, of medicine and engineering. Such applied and interpretative subjects as educational administration and finance of education inevitably focus upon the problems and needs of the systems they serve. Even in the foundation disciplines there is a strong national and system emphasis. Yet, given that we are now all part of a global economic system, that growth and recession interact in complex ways with attitudes towards the present and hopes for the future, and that education is intimately linked with such attitudes and hopes, it is hardly surprising that many tasks and trends *are* common to different societies.

At the most general level, the intellectual climates of free-market and mixed-economy multi-party nations were characterized during the period since the Second World War by a more or less profound cultural pessimism. If we still believed that the best way in which to close a prison is to open a school, that a direct connection exists between rates of participation in education and levels of industrial productivity, and that years of schooling correlate simply and positively with the willingness and ability of a society to value and defend democratic institutions and individual freedom, then education would enjoy higher status and priority, reflected in the standing of those who educate and train its practitioners. But in societies in which participation in primary and secondary education is universal, belief in such simple positive relationships is no longer widespread. The process of education is tainted by association with the reflexiveness and guilt of contemporary consciousness. Sceptical intellectuals of every age have known that the link between knowledge and virtue was not as simple as it looked. Now everyone knows it, and the broad base of political support for the continued extension of education as a self-evident good has to that extent been eroded.

Influential educators could ask in the 1930s, 'Dare the school build a new social order?' Prominent sociologists such as Jean

Floud [18] could point in the early '60s to ways in which schools, assisted by universities committed to the study of education, might counter many of the less creditable characteristics of modern society. But the demographic and economic downturns of the 1970s, coupled with greater sophistication in our understanding of economic and social change, generated doubts about the uncritical acceptance of education as investment. Financial exigency emphasized the need for selectivity and targeting of resources. There was some loss of confidence in the social, political, and economic benefits that flow from non-specific collective and individual investment in education. Liberalism gave way to vocationalism. Institutional and professional autonomy took second place to accountability and central control. Value for money was no longer assumed; it had to be demonstrated.

All this can be seen as part of a wider cultural transition. Georgian civility and Victorian industrial optimism were eroded by post-nuclear despair, exacerbated by difficulties in adjusting public expenditure to the expectations generated by half a century or more of welfare policies in a context of sharp international trade competition and high inflation. In the 1980s government has made a conscious attempt to encourage a more entrepreneurial, risk-taking 'culture of enterprise'.

Families and individual citizens, valuing education as a positional and personal good, persistently place it higher on their agenda of concern than politicians seem prepared to. Its extension and improvement are limited by the inability of governments to face the political costs and administrative complexities of striking a balance of public and private expenditure which would put a realistic price upon training that yields assured private rates of return without prejudicing the educational opportunities of the less well-off. Yet, however much they may now entertain doubts about the value and efficacy of social engineering, politicians, administrators, and individual teachers continue to demonstrate optimism about the ability of education to change individuals, societies, and economies in ways they value and desire.

Such optimism is indeed essential to the educator. It has been argued that the humanities do not humanize, that much so-called social science is covertly ideological, that beyond their laboratories and workplaces scientists are no more objective, rational or disinterested than any other citizen. As individuals and citizens we none the less continue to put our faith in the transmission and the acquisition of worthwhile knowledge, skills, and attitudes as a

70

necessary element in our economic and personal salvation. Formal education remains an essential feature of the civilizing process, and an activity in which increasing proportions of the population, of all ages, take part. It is a proper responsibility of universities to engage, not only in preparing and updating those who teach, but also in the critical examination of all aspects of the processes of teaching and learning, not least how they influence the state and prospects of the economy.

NOTES

1. Department of Education and Science, *Teacher Education and Training: a Report by a Committee of Enquiry appointed by the Secretary of State under the Chairmanship of Lord James of Rusholme* (the James Report), London, 1972.

2. T. Blackstone and A. Crispin, *How Many Teachers? Issues of Policy, Practice and Demography*, London, 1982.

3. V.S. Vance and P.C. Schlechty, 'The distribution of academic ability in the teaching force', *Phi Delta Kappan*, September 1982, p. 26.

4. H.J. Judge, *Graduate Schools of Education: a View from Abroad*, New York, 1982.

5. B. Othaniel Smith, *Design for a School of Pedagogy*, Washington, D.C., 1981, p. 3.

6. H. Gideonse, 'The necessary revolution in teacher education', *Phi Delta Kappan*, September 1982.

7. Carnegie Forum on Education and the Economy, *A Nation Prepared*, Washington, D.C., 1986.

8. Holmes Group, *Tomorrow's Teachers*, East Lansing, Mich., 1986.

9. L. Cremin, 'The problematics of education in the 'eighties', *Oxford Review of Education*, 9, 1 (1983), p. 16.

10. H. Broudy, 'The brightest and the best', *Phi Delta Kappan*, May 1979, p. 644.

11. R.J. Brownhill, *Education and the Nature of Knowledge*, London, 1983.

12. Smith, op. cit., n.5.

13. Department of Education and Science, Circular No. 3/84, 1984.

14. ibid., para. 12.

15. P. Abbs, 'Training spells the death of education', *Guardian*, 5 January 1987.

16. R. Mitchell, *The Graves of Academe*, Boston, Mass., 1982, p. 92.

17. W. Taylor, *Society and the Education of Teachers*, London, 1969.

18. J.E. Floud, 'Teaching in the affluent society', *Yearbook of Education*, London, 1963.

5

Engineering

Geoffrey Sims

The development of engineering on the continent of Europe owes much to Napoleon. It was he who sowed the seeds of the *grandes écoles* in France to cater for the needs of the civil as well as the military engineers that his country needed. This model was rapidly expanded by Germany, and the *Technische Hochschule* came into existence, producing respected and well-educated professional engineers, well matched to the needs of the developing industries of the time. There was no such parallel in Britain. The first chair of engineering at Cambridge was founded in 1875, and not only was engineering seen as a peripheral academic pursuit but the standing of engineering in the academic world was destined to remain low. In sharp contrast, the country at large had enjoyed considerable engineering successes: indeed, the geniuses who inspired British engineering towards the end of the eighteenth century were widely respected; it was from their 'clubability', manifested in the Smeatonian Society, that the Institution of Civil Engineers sprang in 1818 and which laid the firm foundation of professional engineering in Britain. Notwithstanding, engineering was still seen by many of the better-off as an interesting diversion rather than a serious business. The triumphs of the Telfords, the Brunels, and the Stephensons, paralleled by the achievements of people like Watt and Trevithick, had helped to give us a mining industry, a railway system, and a place in capital-goods engineering which was the envy of the world, but this was achieved more on the basis of inspiration and instinct than of systematic education, as noted in an earlier chapter. By the end of the century individual attitudes and market forces were to leave Britain exposed at a time when new technologies were developing apace and requiring a level of educated appreciation which, as yet, just did not exist. Indeed, we remained a country which, when it recognized the problem at all, saw science as the answer to everything and for a century failed to recognize the deep differences between scientific and engineering education needs. Put another way, we had some understanding of the pursuit of truth but failed to realize that scientific method was only a part of the weaponry needed to attack the open-ended problems of which engineering is made up and for which there was seldom a unique solution.

Indeed, it was only relatively late in the twentieth century that these questions started to become the focus of real public attention. It was observed that in Germany, for example, something like seven out of every nine engineers produced by the educational system were employed not in engineering research and development but in essential business support services such as design and marketing. At last people were beginning to ask why it was that the status of the engineer on the Continent was so high while in Britain it remained so low. There are few simple answers to these questions but the brief history outlined in the preceding paragraphs gives some clue as to why things were as they were and why we were to face increasing economic difficulties as technology became increasingly important.

ROUTES TO QUALIFICATION

Until the 1960s the engineering which had developed in the universities had sought to see all engineering as a unity where largely similar curricula could prepare the student for entry to any branch, perhaps with a little specialized fine tuning in the final year. This was the kind of engineering which suited the industry which we had had in the first half of the century, but the complication associated with the thrust of new technology was now demanding substantial specialist knowledge and skills as well. The obvious answer was to lengthen engineering courses to an extent comparable to those already existing on the Continent (which were usually at least five years in length) and to provide specialisms, along with the general training. Sadly this solution found no favour with successive governments, all so preoccupied with keeping public expenditure down that we stayed predominantly with three-year courses, which for the most part became more and more specialized whilst remaining curiously isolated from many of the factors which were of fundamental importance in the real engineering world. Indeed, the movement was so strong that the still much needed 'general' engineer had become something of a rarity by the 1970s.

It is easy to argue that universities should teach engineering principles and that it is for others to build upon those principles throughout a lifetime of experience in industry, but technological change was too rapid for this solution to work effectively. Furthermore the need came into sharpest focus at a time when industry was least prepared, or indeed able, to contribute. It is interesting to contrast the situation at the end of the Second World War with that which pertained some twenty years later. In the late '40s there were a substantial variety of routes to engineering qualification through part-time study, which could be undertaken concurrently with working in the profession. Indeed, many of the more forward-looking firms, most notable of all perhaps Metropolitan-Vickers, had impressively developed graduate apprenticeship schemes through which the newly 'academically-principled' graduate could acquire his earthy industrial experience.

By the late 1960s this flexible situation had disappeared and industry was doing very little to encourage either education or training: it was increasingly all left to the universities. It was a period characterized by much acrimony, about the unworldliness of the universities on the one hand, and about an industry which was always dissatisfied but unable to express what it really needed, on the other. Indeed, it was only at a very much later stage that it became apparent that we would need to rebuild many of the elements of the system which had existed before the war, which enabled people, through part-time study, to update the education which they had received at university, in order to stay in step with the constant stream of new methods and technologies. Further, and of increasing importance, they would need continually to acquire new professional skills to add to their engineering expertise if they were to stay in the race with other countries. Thus the 'new' concept of post-experience vocational education (PEVE) was born, though it developed slowly, partly because of an initial reluctance by government to invest in it, matched only by the diffidence of industry to become involved, for different but rather more complex economic reasons. In fairness it should be acknowledged that, at this stage, federal legislation in Germany had been equally unsuccessful in promoting short-course education, whilst in France, although quite impressive things were happening based on

Napoleon's *grandes écoles* in the universities, for the most part, nothing stirred.

Where, then, were we going and what remained wrong? We had abolished part-time routes to professional qualifications for prestige purposes. We had, with few exceptions, stayed with the concept of the three-year engineering course; so what else was amiss and what could be done about it?

FINNISTON AND THE 'ENGINE OF CHANGE'

Much was expected to develop as a consequence of the Finniston inquiry, which reported in January 1980. The report, *inter alia*, tackled imaginatively and deeply the needs of engineering, the problem of routes to qualification, and the roles of higher educational institutions in the process.

Finniston recognized that the needs of the industry required, for some, a longer graduation period than three years, for which university engineers had long been pressing, whilst for others the three-year route should still be adequate. He also made it clear that there should, as in times past, be open the possibility of transfer between routes, whether part-time or full-time, and that late developers should be able to achieve professional status.

The educational process was envisaged as needing certain common linking elements for all kinds of engineer, in particular a common acquaintance with current workshop technology and materials engineering. These strands should be made compulsory for all courses, to be accredited through the professional bodies, leading to the status of 'chartered engineer' and formal 'registration'.

Further, the government should establish an 'Engineering Authority' whose task it would be to oversee the work of the professional institutions, which would usually remain the accrediting agents, and which would take overall responsibility for the registration of Chartered Engineers.

These proposals were generally welcomed by the universities, not least because they saw in them the hope of obtaining the additional resources which they had for so long felt necessary to perform adequately the task that they saw to be needed for the best of their intake.

After much consultation the 'Authority' in the form of the Engineering Council was set up in November 1981 but most would still be disappointed at the present time with its achievement thus far. That it has sought to play its role as the 'engine of change' that Finniston conceived it to be, few would deny – nor would they disagree with the recommendations of the steady flow of policy papers it has produced. All too sadly and typically, however, its existence in a monetarist age has meant that little, if any, additional resources have been made available for the higher educational institutions as a result of its efforts, and it has not, so far, commanded the respect from government that industry and the educational system had so eagerly hoped for. Its presence remains valuable, but most would wish to see its influence manifested in a more tangible form.

None of this should be taken as arguing that Finniston's impact has been negligible, for considerable change has taken place in the institutions of higher education, though under great difficulty and on what is, for the most part, a sub-optimal scale through lack of resources.

RESEARCH AND INDUSTRIAL CHANGE

As the university system continued to develop and the quality of its students improved so indeed did its research capability but it was also observed, with increasing frequency, that notwithstanding a reasonably substantial national research expenditure by government in the universities little emerged from it which added to the prosperity of the economy, even if we were rather good at winning Nobel Prizes. The all too familiar story of Britain being good at invention and inept at development and exploitation was repeated by government with increasing venom. 'It was of course the fault of the universities', which did not properly prepare their students. In fact it was not particularly fruitful to seek to attribute blame in this situation, for the universities probably did their best within the limits of their capacity at the time. Meanwhile industry at large was so preoccupied with survival that it seldom found the time to look at what part it might be playing in the development or exploitation of research, or indeed in seeking to come to terms with the proposition that the kind of engineer needed for the future was rapidly becoming different from that sought after in the past. Competition, particularly from the Far East, had already reduced, if not terminated, the viability of many of our 'smokestack' industries, whose competitiveness had undoubtedly been reduced, among other things, by the fact that they did not employ very many graduates anyway! What was needed was a genuinely constructive dialogue between higher educational institutions and industry, backed by a genuine willingness on both sides to adapt to an undeniable need. The dialogue sometimes took place, but the *will* to act was often conspicuous by its absence.

On the other side of the coin, the higher-technology industries were less erring in this latter respect, but saw their future best served by larger and larger conglomerates, with the result that Britain was rapidly becoming numerically the smallest employer of labour through medium and small firms in Europe, and whilst the large firms grew larger and larger, for the most part, they were enjoying less and less success in the tough world markets of the time. Clearly generalizations of this kind are unfair to some, but they remain none the less broadly true. The eclipse of the small firm, coupled with the capital structure existing in the country at the time, had done much to damp down the entrepreneurial spirit from which many of our past successes had derived. At the same time the large new conglomerates had in many cases not succeeded in establishing their position in world markets, often as a result of having failed to exploit newly emerging technologies, not uncommonly backed by the belief that the old ones were yet able to support them for a while longer. It was indeed a sorry picture, but let us try to explore what was wrong with their products or salesmanship.

With the advance of the new technologies from the late 1960s onwards more and more importance became attached to reliability in manufacture, and with it came the need to design to higher standards, not just aesthetically but, rather more important, from a sound engineering standpoint. Indeed, design quality, reliability, and most of all cost, became essential attributes for survival. Yet appreciation of these factors alone was not enough unless you had an intelligent, educated marketing force selling ahead of your competitors around the world. Where these factors were appreciated success was still achieved, but overall there was a long persistence of outdated attitudes which did not make it easy for traditional manufacturers to come together in a way which enabled them to compete with some of the 'cheaper' giants existing in other parts of the world.

A new attitude was also needed on the part of much of our industry towards investment. Once again it was the older industries which were slow to respond, having been used to the expectation of long-period returns on capital invested and consequently having become reluctant to indulge in 'unnecessary' investment in new processes and equipment. The relatively sudden appearance of new technologies like micro-electronics, with the coupled benefit of the micro-computer, the rapid rise in importance of computer-aided design and computer-aided manufacture, all centring around the newly formed all-embracing concept of information technology, had left an economically starved industry, not only breathless but often bankrupt.

Oddly, economic factors apart, the universities had frequently responded more rapidly to these changes than had industry. Many universities were turning out students who knew about micro-technology and its importance, who were certainly conversant with computer applications and, in many cases, had had experience of computer-aided design and manufacture. It is, however, one thing to learn about these things in a university in a simulated atmosphere of industrial realism; however realistic an atmosphere can be contrived, it is another to apply them in the hard world of industry in the face of real market intelligence, real economic pressure, and real competition. It is true that there were some notable and successful experiments in getting the two sides together, of which the Teaching Company Scheme, referred to in chapter 2, was one of the most successful. Further, those universities which were inclined that way were becoming inundated with industrial enquiries as to how industry could use the new technology for its own purposes. Many useful collaborations grew from these contacts, and there were few universities which did not make some effort at least in the direction of extending their expertise and facilities towards industry. Unfortunately the process did not always occur quite as effectively the other way round, and the author recalls, with some sadness, having to listen to an industrialist saying to him, on one occasion, 'Do you really mean you want me to make my men available to spend time taking part in the education in your university when they could be doing something useful and productive in industry?'

WEAKNESSES

It is not easy, with hindsight, to see what the universities could have done to improve the situation on their own. It is true that their teaching often lacked the realism that goes with the experience of the constraints imposed by market costs, reliability, capital investment, saleability, and so on. It is true also that the fascination of many academics with the newest of technologies caused them to illustrate their basic principles with examples which were often beyond the 'state of the art' of the industry of the day. Yet would the universities have really helped had they merely taught 'state of the art' technology which was already rapidly dating? For though it might have better matched the immediate needs of the industry concerned, it would not have opened the minds of its recipients to the more imaginative possibilities which might lie ahead. The author remains convinced that it could only have been through some kind of jointly devised process, by which students were introduced to the realities of industry as part of their course at appropriate stages, that we could have achieved a more satisfactory situation. This last statement should not necessarily be taken as adumbration of the virtues of sandwich courses, which certainly fulfilled one kind of need, but they were seldom as well 'integrated', in terms of the complementarity of the training process and the educational components, as might have been desired. Further, industry remained notoriously bad at taking advantage of the attributes of the qualified scientists and engineers which it employed and only slowly came to the conclusion that it not only needed inventors and, above all, designers of the highest class, but that people of comparable intelligence, knowledge, and ability were essential to look after all the complexities of the marketing side of their products as well. Indeed, many a promising high-technology firm has failed because of its inability to educate the market, into which it was trying to sell, that it had a need for its products. The entrenched attitudes of some industries still make this a major problem for the smaller high-technology firm seeking to establish itself in the face of major competition from more technologically aware countries.

THE PROBLEMS OF TECHNOLOGY TRANSFER

There is another important aspect of this picture, relating to the utilization of university research, which, as I have indicated earlier, had become more and more application-oriented as time went on. What then happened to the results of most of this research? I suppose that the short answer is that it was reported to conferences, or appeared in papers in learned journals which many of those in industry had little time to read. Indeed, even if they had been read and digested, there was often inevitably a wide gulf between the bright idea as it emerged from its chrysalis in the university and the fully formed butterfly which might one day charm the world. It was and still is the so-called 'pre-competitive' phase which is often the most expensive in terms of investment in the new product, and it remains the gap which we most often signally fail to bridge. Few universities had the design ability to take their ideas to the point of producing genuinely marketable products, and indeed much of their research at its best could only have been considered as a part-contribution to anything large and ambitious. Thus much potentially 'applicable' research ended in sterility. On the industrial side, at the same time, costs had frequently been so trimmed, as a result of high-wage policies and other inflationary forces, that far too little attention was given to providing development facilities which were capable of taking such advanced ideas forward. With some of the bigger firms there was also a strong belief that 'industry alone knew how to do it', and could always do it better than the universities anyway, resulting in a reluctance even to spend time discussing the issues. Whilst as a generalization this attitude could claim some justification, that justification was not without exceptions! Happily, by the 1980s, there were significant signs of a much more fruitful interaction, though many fundamental links yet remained to be forged – among them many in the all-embracing area of design.

The design problem, though the subject of many previous, less incisive reports, was perhaps most clearly and constructively discussed in the Lickley Report, published by the Science and Engineering Research Council (SERC) in 1983. Lickley himself, a greatly experienced industrial designer, went to some pains to take evidence from industry and the universities on the subject and concluded, not surprisingly, that the solution to the grave designer shortage could not be achieved by either party on its own. But would industry be prepared to release its best, most up-to-date designers to work with the universities in educating the next generation? If the designers were not at the forefront in the use of the new technology they were not going to be of much use to the universities, and if they were *au courant* they could be ill spared. In the universities there were a growing number of people who were familiar with the forefront technology but had never had to design in the industrial context, and a marriage was clearly needed. As so often, policy was slow to evolve, and whilst some progress was made, much remains to be done. It was not without precedent that the directorate within the SERC, which Lickley had recommended to stimulate the process through directed awards similar to the successful pattern already used for marine technology and polymer engineering, failed to materialize. The reason was partly lack of finance, but this in itself was, in part, a consequence of the ponderousness of the process by which discussions on any matter affecting the budgets of more than one government department usually proceed. In the end the concept of the directorate was condensed to the appointment of a single design co-ordinator who, though experienced and competent, could only function within the limits of one man's energies, however prodigious.

NEW MACHINERY

As a result of encouragement from many sources, not least from government, there had from the late 1960s onwards been an increasing tendency for universities to set up industrial advisory services. In the early days many of these showed signs of amateurism, if not naïvety, but hard experience taught the better of them how to offer services that industry really needed and could utilize. Specialist advisory services in areas like sound and vibration research, metallurgy, electronics, and many others, began to find a real presence in universities, often employing their own staff to offer advice, consultancy and an ability to achieve genuine technology transfer into industry. All these activities had to be financed from somewhere, and most had to be pump-primed from some external source. Certain of the foundations, and from time to time ministries (if not on a particularly generous scale), made resources available and there is now a significant array of industrial services of this sort available from many universities. Most of the industries that use them seem well pleased, though there are universities which continue to remain in detached isolation and often pay a price for so doing. It would be arrogant to pretend that the universities had all the answers, but at least they had some, and often they were valuable. Some universities founded consultancy companies, attempting at times quite ambitious projects such as the complete ergodynamic redesign of the standard British fire engine (which has now been in production for some ten years or more).

Others, with the passage of time, found that they were in a position to contemplate setting up companies, or holding companies, through which their own inventions could be exploited. Such ideas were not original, for this had been happening in the United States following the massive sums invested in the universities for research during the war. It was this investment, primarily required for military purposes, that had made possible the multitude of small-firm developments and had created a climate for later civil developments of a like 'science park' kind: indeed, it was from these small-firm 'seeds' that many of the present major contributors to the US economy have grown. In Europe too the concept had taken root, if somewhat later, and the University of Louvain, for example, had founded a development company from which spin-off companies were steadily being formed to exploit university inventions. There, as in Britain, most of the companies concerned were small in scale, but at a time when job creation is a national priority even small firms make their contribution, and some of these ventures will undoubtedly grow substantially, given time.

Many universities had thus, at last, become conscious that if technology transfer from the research bench to the market place was to occur they were going to have to do a lot of the pushing themselves. This was perhaps more consonant with the spirit of the times than might at first have seemed likely, but increasingly the need to encourage 'entrepreneurialism', as it was rather inaccurately called, was beginning to be recognized. Yesterday's large old firms were dying and therefore new firms needed to be seeded, some of which would grow in time to take their place. In 1983 Britain had proportionately fewer firms with under 200 employees than any other developed country, which in itself tells a story.

THE SMALL-FIRM PROBLEM

For Britain, in particular, the small firm had always presented problems. Few small firms employed graduates, and many of them, e.g. single-product companies which made a good living producing piece parts for larger manufacturers, felt no need to do so. Thus overheads were kept to a minimum and there was little investment in forward thinking, a dangerous position to be in, in a rapidly changing technological world. Much of the earlier university effort to move closer to industry had involved attempts to set up machinery for the solution of small firms' problems. This not infrequently benefited the small firms, but not by any means in all cases. Above all, it educated the universities to recognize that people in the small firms of the time did not often think as university graduates think, and furthermore were often reluctant to accept the undoubtedly sound solutions which were being offered by their university counterparts. It was therefore necessary – and indeed it still remains necessary today – to find improved mechanisms whereby small firms and universities could interact in ways calculated to stimulate mutual confidence and to result in a genuine meeting of minds. The problem is still mainly one of effective communication, but it has to be communication conducted in an atmosphere of shared humility! Many universities attempt this through young executives' clubs, managing directors' clubs, and the like, and these achieve a useful basic purpose, that of getting to know one another. It is only when confidence is established that the small firm is likely to take very much notice of any technical advice, or offer of facilities, from universities. 'Gateway' schemes which enable small firms to take advantage of graduate skills, on a sampling basis, represent a constructive and important step forward, but need to be continued over an extended period if a real impact is to be made on a sufficient scale.

SCIENCE PARKS

I have, thus far, omitted to refer to 'science parks', which first arose as a part manifestation of the heavy funding of many universities in the United States during the war years. After the war many of those who had been working in forefront high-technology research chose to establish businesses based on that research in close proximity to the parent university. Similarly Route 128 became famous in the United States for its concentration of high-technology firms, most of which were linked to 'parent university' interests. Clearly the concept was bound to find its way to Europe in time, and in Britain the Cambridge Science Park was deemed a great success. Other science parks were formed, to the extent that there are now some thirty in existence, but their success is nothing like so clearly manifest. Recent experience suggests that, even given favourable conditions, e.g. the provision of adequate buildings and low interest rates, there is seldom a rush to fill them with new enterprises. When those enterprises do come, they are unlikely to be 'high-technology-associated'. By far the most important factor, the surveys conclude, is the general ambience of the location; if in some cases the high technology which may be available in the university is an attraction, it is not necessarily the primary magnet of the development.

It is difficult at this time to try to deduce too much from this analysis but it is probable that the scale of investment in university technology in Britain, and indeed in much of Europe also, is not such that it can reproduce the spectacular success of the US developments. Further, in Britain, the most successful ventures are likely to take place where local authorities are prepared to give rating concessions to firms establishing themselves on the park, or where the university itself has acquired land or participated in property development on the basis of long-term, low-interest-rate loans. These are not available in all parts of the country, and it is this factor alone which has dissuaded some universities from going forward with the science park concept, persuading them, rather, to choose other means, such as the development of occasional spin-off companies as and when they showed signs of becoming viable.

Other factors too are inhibitory when it comes to setting up new high-technology company developments. Interest rates, and the structure of the capital market in Britain, are such that with the effective repayment periods currently on offer it is seldom a paying proposition to found a business unless you already have a ready-marketable product and proven market. It is possible to achieve this in sectors of the software and other industries but more rarely so in the case of those based in manufactured products. Indeed, until we find an answer to the basic problem to which I have already referred – the need to achieve sufficient product development following laboratory innovation – things are likely to remain as they are. It is not that there is a shortage of venture capital available but that British venture capitalists in what is, in comparison with the USA, a low-volume business are inclined to be less 'venturesome', preferring to invest in the more secure pastures of business expansions and management buy-outs rather than the marshier lands of business start-ups.

MORE ENGINEERS?

But what of the future? At the time of writing, government attitudes to the universities are not particularly encouraging. It sees them as expensive and often primarily as a vehicle for the education of the maximum possible number of young people at lower cost. The country is seen, none the less, to need more engineers and scientists, and provided we produce them all will be well. From the university standpoint there is no reluctance to attempt the task, but in these times the production of tomorrow's good engineers requires facilities of a kind that rarely exist, either in universities or for that matter in much of industry. Also, if the task is to be done properly, it is a highly labour-intensive process, needing the involvement of people at the forefront of design development. In other spheres – for example, the world of the medical schools – the labour-intensive nature is readily accepted because human life is at stake. Notwithstanding, comparable arguments do not seem to cut much ice when it is only the economy which is at issue, even if, at the end of the day, it is only a prosperous economy that helps to sustain them and through them the preservation of human life. There is no way that the university system can continue to produce quality products whilst the relentless attrition of its base funding continues.

Once again, however, this is but half the story, for while government on the one hand acknowledges that we need more engineers, the truth of the matter is that already the universities probably produce sufficient engineers to meet the economic need. Many of them, however, are attracted to work anywhere *but* the engineering industry because of the low rewards which are available to them as professional engineers. It is to be hoped that we may be observing a transient phenomenon, but even if this is so it remains an extremely dangerous one: for example, one could quote the case of an extremely distinguished, world-ranking, engineering department in the University of London where no fewer than 85 per cent of its graduates take jobs in the City rather than in engineering. It is not a question of disenchantment with the subject, merely a matter of rewards and career prospects. More generally, as already stated, it is not uncommon for universities to see some 50 per cent of their engineers going into accountancy or other professions at the end of their course because that is where the material rewards are. It is not, so far as one can judge, that they have found their university experience of engineering unrewarding in itself, merely that in a materialistic society they see career prospects which, for the moment, are at their most attractive when they involve the direct processing of money as opposed to products.

This is a problem that industry alone can solve. Indeed, the overhead on most projects which accrues from the salaries of the engineers employed is such a small part of the total cost of manufacture and marketing that doubling those salaries would probably not affect the ultimate product selling price very much. In such altered circumstances the universities, even at their present reduced level of funding, would probably be seen as largely satisfying the national need.

6

Medicine

R.E. Coupland

The accusation of special pleading is an abiding memory of those who have served, to safeguard the interests of the minority group, on committees composed of nominees of both health authorities and universities and even on inter-faculty university committees. Indeed, using 'special' in the sense of relating to activities additional to ordinary ones, it is not an inappropriate description, even though the term is usually used in a dismissive way.

With the current rate of scientific and professional advance in medicine (and dentistry), it is essential that undergraduate courses should be both vocational and educational. They should also be recognized as the beginning of a continuing exercise that must extend throughout the lifetime of the individual practitioner. Such an outcome can be achieved only if those responsible for undergraduate medical education and for health care work together in partnership to achieve the common goal of a high standard of health care for each individual in the United Kingdom.

Currently, progress is often hampered by the lack of understanding of planners and managers of needs and aims. The following attempts to present a brief account of the evolution of the current system of medical education and health services in Britain, as well as the professional and financial constraints within which the university component must operate.

HISTORICAL

Man's concern about health and the wish of those afflicted for cure, relief, or comfort is evident throughout recorded history. In medieval times a theoretical knowledge of medicine was largely restricted to the clergy and clerks in monasteries and ancient universities; the more practical application of cures or remedies was conducted by individuals sometimes called leechers, who had trained by apprenticeship.

For generations the division between the more theoretical and more practical aspects of medical practice persisted, leading to the identification of physicians, who diagnosed, prescribed, and prognosed; barber surgeons, who cut, bled, dressed wounds, and extracted teeth; and apothecaries, who were concerned with dispensing herbal and other medicines.

As the population grew and urbanization occurred medical corporations developed in prosperous towns and cities, leading to the formation of guilds of barber surgeons, apothecaries (who were initially members of grocers' guilds), and physicians.

For many years medical education and examinations were often organized and conducted separately, without formal links. During the seventeenth century colleges of physicians in Edinburgh and London [1] expected that those applying for apprenticeship training leading to examinations would be graduates of Scottish universities, Oxford or Cambridge, or quite often of a university in Western Europe (Bologna, Padua, Leyden, etc.).

With the realization of the importance of a knowledge of anatomy, physiology and morbid anatomy in the rational understanding and delivery of medicine, more formal courses began to evolve and were provided often by private schools in London, Edinburgh and Glasgow which had variable links with adjacent hospitals.

The Apothecaries Act, 1815, was a significant landmark in medical education in Britain, as it made attendance at specific courses of lectures compulsory for student apothecaries and surgical students prior to entry for qualifying examinations. This requirement was followed by an expansion in the number of medical teachers throughout the country, but especially in London, leading within the next few years to the formation of further medical schools, both in London (the existing schools were St Thomas's, St Bartholomew's, Guy's, and the London Hospital) [2] and in the provinces, including Birmingham and Sheffield (1828), Leeds (1831), Newcastle upon Tyne (1832), Bristol (1833), and Liverpool (1834).[3] Each published a comprehensive curriculum. They were staffed by local physicians, surgeons, and obstetricians, sometimes supplemented, with respect to chemistry and botany, by teachers at local colleges of education.

When the University of London was founded in 1836 it had the power to examine and confer degrees upon students attending approved institutions within the United Kingdom. Approved colleges in provincial cities made use of this dispensation and started to prepare students to take the external London degree. In 1858 the condition regarding attendance at approved institutions was relaxed by London University for all except medical students.

Concern about the standard of medical education and the involvement in medical practice of unqualified individuals led to legislation in the form of the Medical Act, 1858, which set up the General Council of Medical Education and Registration of the United Kingdom; since 1951 this body has been officially known as the General Medical Council (GMC). Its prime duties were: (1) to compile and publish annually *The Medical Register*, in order to enable the public to distinguish qualified from unqualified practitioners; (2) to have responsibility for overseeing standards of medical education in the licensing bodies approved; and (3) to publish a reliable pharmacopoeia. The council was also authorized to erase from the register the name of any practitioner convicted of a criminal offence, or judged 'to have been guilty of infamous conduct in any professional respect'. [4] With respect to medical education, the Act empowered the GMC to ask licensing bodies (nineteen at the time) to provide full information about current courses of study and examinations and to send visitors to attend and report upon any examinations held by the bodies.

By comparison with the remainder of Western Europe, England was slow to incorporate the rapidly developing natural sciences and natural philosophy within medical education. Scotland was, however, further advanced in this respect. During the second half of the nineteenth century the importance of science became more widely acknowledged, and local education colleges, medical schools, and teaching hospitals were drawn together in the provision of medical education. Ultimately the local colleges and medical schools were amalgamated to form university colleges. They were established by royal charter towards the end of the century and survived to achieve university status. The older English civic universities with medical schools were founded prior to the Second World War and include Birmingham, Bristol, Leeds, Liverpool, Manchester, Newcastle, and Sheffield, while Nottingham, Southampton, and Leicester were founded subsequently. In Scotland the first chairs in the medical school in Dundee can trace their foundation back to 1887, when pre-clinical departments were established within University College, Dundee. In 1897 University College became part of the University of St Andrews and was renamed Queen's College in 1954. In 1967 Queen's College separated from St Andrews, forming the independent University of Dundee.

At present there are four university medical schools in Scotland, twelve English provincial schools, schools in Wales (Cardiff) and Belfast, while in London, of the former twelve medical schools, some exist independently and some are amalgamated to a varying degree with other medical schools or non-medical university colleges. St Andrews still possesses a pre-clinical medical school and graduates move mainly to Manchester for clinical medical education.

THE ROLE OF THE GENERAL MEDICAL COUNCIL IN MEDICAL EDUCATION

Since its foundation in 1858 the responsibilities and size of the council have expanded according to need and a succession of Medical Acts. There are now some ninety-five members, approximately half of whom are elected by members of the profession. The others include lay members and one individual appointed by each of the licensing bodies, including universities with medical schools, the Society of Apothecaries, and specialist royal colleges and faculties. Members are elected to GMC committees yearly.

Until 1953 it sufficed for registration that the applicant should have passed the qualifying examinations of a licensing body in medicine, surgery, and midwifery.[5] However, under the Medical Act, 1950 (since 1 January 1953), anyone obtaining a registrable qualification must subsequently take approved resident appointments for a period of twelve months as a pre-registration house officer before applying for full registration. Acceptable combinations of experience in general medicine and surgery and in clinical specialties during the pre-registration period are set out in *Recommendations on Basic Medical Education.*[6]

Prior to 1978 the Medical Acts specified that the standard of proficiency of candidates at the qualifying examinations should be 'such as sufficiently to guarantee the possession of knowledge and skill requisite for the efficient practice of Medicine, Surgery and Midwifery'.[7] The Medical Act of 1978 changed this, substituting the need for a 'prescribed knowledge and skill' at the time of qualification and a 'prescribed pattern of experience' during the pre-registration year and prior to registration. The nature and extent of the knowledge and experience are prescribed by the Education Committee of the GMC.

Visitors are sent to medical schools, under the terms of the Medical Act of 1950, approximately every five years. Their observations and findings are presented as reports and recommendations to council, and copies are sent to the licensing body concerned.

LOCAL HEALTH SERVICES AND HOSPITALS [8]

Although hospitals have been in existence in Britain since Roman times, initially they were associated with monasteries, priories, and cathedrals. During the Middle Ages a close working association with local physicians, surgeons, and apothecaries was established.

The eighteenth century saw the beginning of the voluntary hospital movement in Britain, and following the Continental pattern hospitals were provided for the sick poor and funded primarily by voluntary contributions. During the eighteenth century the majority of London teaching hospitals were founded. In the provinces similar institutions were established in centres of population and in county towns. Following the passing of the Sanitary Act, 1866, and Public Health Act, 1875, two important milestones with respect to the development of health care, Poor Law infirmaries were established by local authorities. The nineteenth century also witnessed the founding of many specialist hospitals, especially in London. However, the voluntary hospitals were the ones mainly used for clinical teaching.

During the early twentieth century it became apparent that the number of hospital beds was inadequate for population needs, and also that they could not be adequately financed by voluntary contributions alone. Shortly after the First World War a committee set up by the Minister of Health reported that 378 of 672 voluntary hospitals were in debt. The Local Government Act, 1927, gave local authorities wider powers to provide hospitals and encouraged co-operation with voluntary hospitals to meet demand. In 1935 a commission under the chairmanship of Viscount Sankey was established to enquire into the state of the voluntary hospitals. Its report, published in 1937, recommended that the country should be divided into hospital regions, with regional councils to supervise work and needs, the regional councils to be responsible to a central council. It also recommended that regional funds should be created for the benefit of all hospitals, finance being derived from central government, from local authorities, and from voluntary contributions.

During the Second World War the coalition government announced its intention to establish a comprehensive health service, and in 1944 a White Paper entitled *A National Health Service* was published to stimulate discussion of a plan that would enable everyone 'to obtain medical advice and treatment .... without charge'. The suggestion was that the service should be based on the existing local government scheme, but with voluntary (including teaching) hospitals continuing to raise a substantial part of their own finance in order to preserve their independence within the service.

Following the general election of 1945 the Labour government introduced a Bill transferring municipal and voluntary hospitals to State ownership and grouping them for administrative purposes into regions under appointed regional hospital boards with voluntary membership. Provision was also made for regions to be divided into areas and districts for local management, with hospital administration being the responsibility of Hospital Management Committees. The Bill received the royal assent in November 1946 and on 5 July 1948 the National Health Service came into being.

During the 1940s more extensive use had been made of municipal hospitals for teaching purposes to complement and supplement the experience obtained within teaching voluntary hospitals. Profound changes in practice and in particular in therapy followed the major advances in medical science during the war years, stimulating an increase in clinical research. This led to the establishment of clinical academic departments in universities, with full-time staff who were given honorary clinical appointments at appropriate levels of seniority in the health service. Previously, although full-time clinical academic chairs had existed in the Scottish universities, at Oxford, and in the provincial universities, full-time academic staff were usually limited to basic medical science departments (Anatomy, Physiology, and later Pharmacology and Biochemistry), Pathology, and Bacteriology. Honorary academic appointments were given to local individuals who were senior honorary consultant clinicians at the teaching hospitals; professional titles had usually been restricted to major disciplines (medicine, surgery, and obstetrics). However, all honorary consultants in teaching hospitals participated fully in clinical teaching of medical undergraduates.

When the new Act came into effect, establishing fourteen English regions, it introduced a system of government for teaching hospitals in England and Wales different from that which was applied to those that were essentially non-teaching. Each teaching group functioned under the control of a board of governors which was responsible direct to the Minister of Health, without statutory connections with the regional hospital board (RHB). The other hospitals were responsible to the RHB. This arrangement created problems, since ever increasing use was being made of other hospitals for teaching purposes and the divided responsibilities hindered the establishment of co-ordinated health care in the district. In Scotland all hospitals, including teaching hospitals, came under the control of one of the fifteen health boards and Scottish universities were allowed to nominate up to one-fifth of the members of boards of hospitals used for clinical teaching.

The priorities of the early 1950s with respect to health were the improvement of medical care and facilities throughout the country and the maintenance of standards of medical education without, at the same time, increasing the degree of deprivation in non-teaching districts.

Following the publication of the Willink Report in 1957,[9] which mistakenly concluded that there was overproduction of medical graduates, the national intake of medical students was reduced and cuts made in the funding of universities with medical schools. In the early 1960s, with the NHS approaching crisis point regarding medical staffing, and with many services largely dependent on recent overseas immigrants, the Department of Health decided health needs could be met only by increasing the output of UK-trained doctors. Subsequently the decision to found three new medical schools was taken (Nottingham, Southampton, and Leicester).

The ministerial announcement relating to Nottingham was made in 1964 and shortly afterwards the University of Nottingham established the Medical School Advisory Committee, under the chairmanship of the late Sir George Pickering (Regius Professor of Medicine at Oxford University), to offer advice and make recommendations relating to medical education, teaching, and research, the best arrangements for the nature and layout of buildings required, and about the university's administrative relationship with the bodies concerned. The Pickering Report [10] suggested that the new teaching hospitals should be governed by a body constituted jointly by the local health authority (Sheffield Regional Hospital Board) and the University of Nottingham as equal partners and financed by the University Grants Committee and the Ministry of Health.

In consequence of the failure of the hospital board and the university to agree on the composition and organization of the governing body or the administration of the new teaching hospital, responsibility for management was vested in the regional hospital board, the composition of which was modified to include university representation. Decisions with respect to the running of the hospital were taken by the hospital management committee, composed of members representing the university, the RHB, and the chief officers of the hospital – two-fifths of members being nominated by the university.

Subsequent to the reorganization of the NHS in 1974, all boards of governors of teaching hospitals and hospital management committees were abolished and a three-tier system was introduced (region, area, and district), each group of teaching hospitals in a locality becoming the responsibility of area health authorities (teaching), with the university concerned nominating two of the members of the area health authority and one member of the regional authority. In addition, joint liaison committees were appointed between universities and the region and the area. Boards of governors were retained only in postgraduate teaching hospitals and institutions belonging to the University of London. Following the publication of the report of the Royal Commission on the NHS and the consultative paper *Patients First* in 1979,[11] the health services were reorganized, with the abolition of areas but retaining regions and modified districts. Universities and teaching hospitals established similar associations with their districts as they had previously had with areas, and regional associations remained more or less as before.

The Griffiths management inquiry and its report in 1984 to the House of Commons Social Services Committee led to a further reorganization, with the introduction of industrial/commercial-style management and the appointment of general managers at regional, district, and unit levels. An English university nominated one member of the regional health authority and two members of the district health authority. In addition to representation on these statutory bodies, by local arrangement there is variable but usually extensive cross-representation of health authority officers and clinical consultants on university committees, including faculty boards and development committees, and of university academic staff on a variety of NHS committees, including the hospital medical executive, district staffing, manpower, regional medical and regional research committees, and ethical committees. Furthermore, the university representatives on the regional and district health authorities also serve on a number of sub-committees. Thus a great amount of time and effort is put in at the local level to ensure the harmonious integration of input from university and NHS with respect to the provision of both health care and medical education.

STUDENT NUMBERS

In 1944 the Goodenough Committee[12] suggested that a total intake of 2,500 students per year would be appropriate to the needs in terms of medical graduates of a population of 47.5 million. However, in 1957 the health departments, alarmed by escalating costs within the service, appointed a committee to consider the 'Future Numbers of Medical Practitioners and the Appropriate Intake of Medical Students'. The Willink Committee[13] recommended a temporary reduction in intake in order to avoid the risk of a situation developing where medical practitioners would be surplus to need. By 1964 only 1,500 were graduating yearly, and shortages were apparent in primary health care and hospital services;[14] furthermore the situation was being aggravated by a substantial loss of graduates by emigration.

This problem was addressed by the Royal Commission on Medical Education,[15] under the chairmanship of Lord Todd, who estimated a need for 78,100 doctors in 1975, 96,400 in 1985 and 119,800 by 1995, based not only on population, which it was estimated might grow from 60.5 million to 66.5 million during the decade 1985–95, but also on likely requirements for medical care. The recommendations of the Royal Commission relating to the annual intake of students are reproduced in Table 6.1. The levels were attainable only if the intake of existing medical schools was increased and new ones (six were recommended) were established. In the event, however, only three new schools have been established and none has attained the Todd target intake of approximately 200 students per year. However, with intakes of

95

Table 6.1 Average annual intake of British-resident students recommended,1960–89, and resulting annual output of graduates, 1965–94[2]

Year of entry	Average annual intake recommended	Year of graduation	Estimated annual number of graduates
1960–64	(2,030)	1965–69	1,830
1965–69	2,600	1970–74	2,350
1970–74	3,500	1975–79	3,150
1975–79	4,300	1980–84	3,850
1980–84	4,700	1985–89	4,250
1985–89	5,000	1990–94	4,500

Source: Royal Commission on Medical Education, 1965–8, *Report*, London, 1968.

between 120 and 140 per year in Leicester, Southampton, and Nottingham and expansion in existing schools the government-modified Todd target intake of 4,087 for Great Britain, including overseas students, has almost been achieved, with the intake during the past five years varying from 3,938 to 3,994. Overseas students have accounted for 4–5 per cent of the total, the remainder being home-based, European Community nationals (very few) or individuals having recent domicile (three years' residence in the UK for a purpose other than education). In 1981 the UGC froze the intake of various medical schools at the level of the previous year (Table 6.2) and this intake has been more or less maintained since, with Leeds, Leicester, Liverpool, Nottingham, Newcastle, and Aberdeen being below the Todd target level.

Currently a further review of the annual intake of medical students is under way at the DHSS in an attempt to gear the output of medical schools to need in the health services. The recommendations will no doubt take note of need in the hospital and community health services in the light of changes consequent upon acceptance, at least in principle, of recommendations made in *Achieving a Balance*, [16] published by the DHSS in 1986. These essentially aim to link the number of junior doctors undergoing specialist training at senior registrar and registrar levels to the number of consultant posts available, recommend a small increase in senior house officer posts and the introduction of a non-training intermediate-level hospital service post. However, since some 50

Table 6.2 Revised intake target of medical schools in Great Britain and Northern Ireland

Birmingham	160	Southampton	130
Bristol	120	Aberdeen	150
Leeds	220	Dundee	110
Leicester	144	Edinburgh	200
Liverpool	150	Glasgow	220
London	1,200	St Andrews	75
Manchester	200	University of Wales School	150
Nottingham	192	of Medicine	
Oxford		Queen's University of	150
Sheffield	150	Belfast	

per cent of medical graduates ultimately enter general practice, it is essential that the family practitioner services are also appraised and, hopefully, brought into line with other parts of the profession with regard to normal retirement age, which is currently not specified.

To date the Joint Planning Advisory Committee (JPAC) of the DHSS has made recommendations regarding the appropriate number of senior registrars in various specialties, and regions have been notified. Regional JPAC committees have been set up to advise on the distribution of posts between NHS units and clinical academic units within health districts. Attention is now turning to the registrar grades, which, it is recommended, will be divided into regional posts and district posts. The former are intended to be held by individuals who will seek a consultant career in the UK, while the district registrar posts will be used primarily for the training of overseas graduates. A major concern of all involved in clinical academic medicine is the relatively short time (two years) acceptable for working as a regional registrar and the major reduction proposed in the number of posts, since for many years the period spent as a registrar or as a clinical lecturer with honorary registrar status has been considered to be that most appropriate for the acquisition of knowledge and skills required for research and involvement in a major research project. Curtailment of proper training in clinical research will inevitably in the long term result in a reduction in the standard of practice in the Health Service.

Table 6.3 Throughput and costs of Trent Regional Hospitals 1985–6[5]

Hospital	Average No. available beds	Average case stay (days)	Net total in-patient per case (£)	Out-patient cost per attendance (£)
Non-teaching				
1	464	6·7	642.60	21.98
2	485	7·0	689.67	26.81
3	440	6·5	608.40	26.63
4	821	6·8	528.31	18.60
Teaching				
1	979	5·9	618.25	25.29
2	904	6·6	728.81	22.79
3	1,245	6·4	663.03	27.63
4	701	8·3	942.28	26.15

Source: Trent Regional Health Authority, 'Summary of Patient Costs and Unit Costs', 1986.

During the past ten years problems have arisen in various schools as a result of the planning and implementation of developments designed to meet the target figures when expected increases in annual intake failed to materialize owing to sudden changes in policy. However, provided targets are set, preferably, five years in advance and adhered to, similar problems should be avoided or minimized as a result of the new system of funding introduced by the University Grants Committee in 1985, since this is geared mainly to student numbers and is less influenced by historic factors.

INTRINSIC COST OF MEDICAL EDUCATION

The difficulties inherent in obtaining a realistic estimate of the cost per student of medical education is well presented in the report of the Royal Commission of 1968.[17] With respect to practically all parameters educated guesstimates must be made, more especially since GMC recommendations for better integration of clinical and pre-clinical phases of education have been superimposed upon the complexity of the highly successful 'knock-for-knock'

Table 6.4 Throughput and costs of provincial and London teaching hospitals, 1985–6

	Provincial	London
Staffed beds:		
Total	12,452	8,943
Range	331–1,245	316–858
Average stay per case (days)	7.44	8.54
Average total cost per in-patient per day (£)	109.16	125.46
Cost range	91.23–129.16	98.78–149.70
Average cost per out-patient attendance	27.32	29.07
Out-patient attendance/new patient ratio	4.53	4.99

Source: *Teaching Hospital Statistics, 1985-86, Actuals,* Statistical Service, Chartered Institute of Public Finance and Accountancy.

arrangements that have existed between universities with medical schools and the NHS.

In the mid-1960s the average cost per medical graduate was £6,650, and this excluded indirect hospital costs, which if included would have taken the figure up to the £10,000–£11,000 calculated by Hill.[18] With the general index of retail prices and purchasing power of the pound showing a sixfold change between 1965 and 1984, this would imply a current cost per graduate of £60,000–£70,000, which must be supplemented by £12,500 derived from local authorities or other sources for living costs.

As observed by the Royal Commission, these guesstimates and calculations took no account of capital costs relating to new buildings or their modification to meet the changing needs of medical education. Furthermore, the significance of Hill's estimates with respect to differences in teaching and non-teaching hospitals of comparable size and catchment population is difficult to evaluate in the light of the variations in environment, general services available, and estate management costs in different centres. These are well illustrated (Table 6.3) by comparing costs *per in-patient case* in four non-teaching acute hospitals having 400–850 beds and in four teaching hospitals with over 700 beds in the Trent region catering for mixed urban and rural populations in the year 1985–6.

Clearly there are substantial differences between hospitals in a particular region and between provincial and London teaching hospitals (Table 6.4). It is also evident that in Trent efficiency as judged by average case stay is better in three out of four of the teaching hospitals than in non-teaching hospitals, but this may reflect inadequate staffing levels in the latter.

STAFFING

According to the UGC[19] in 1985–6 there were in total 7,802 full-time academic staff in England and Wales in cost centre Medicine, Dentistry, and Health, 1,288 in Scotland and 216 in Northern Ireland. Since the old subject classification (Group 11) included medicine, dentistry, pharmacy, pharmacology, and other studies allied to health, these numbers represent inflated values for medicine alone. By comparison, the new classification introduced in 1985, Group 1, Medicine and Dentistry, and including pre-clinical and clinical components, underestimates the number unless institutions are careful to include the proportion of staff (Full Time Equivalent) in anatomy and physiology (cost centre 04), pharmacology (cost centre 05), and biochemistry (09) departments deemed to be concerned solely with medical or dental education under the heading pre-clinical. The new classification does, however, allow one to identify the number of university staff involved in clinical medicine.

From the UGC *University Statistics*[20] the student/staff ratio and unit costs per FTE student in clinical medicine can be calculated (Table 6.5). The new cost centre classification does not allow meaningful estimates to be made of unit costs for pre-clinical medical students, though the majority of departments involved probably have ratios of 10:1 or 11:1. From Table 6.5 it is apparent that although unit costs are similar in England, Wales and Scotland

Table 6.5 Student/staff ratio (SSR) and unit costs in clinical medicine, 1985–6

Country	PTE student load	Staff wholly university-funded	Student/ staff rate	Unit cost £
England	13,492	1,940	7·0	6,575
Wales	522	99	5·3	6,799
Scotland	2,789	395	7·1	6,814

Source: University Grants Committee, *University Statistics 1985-86*, III, *Finance*, Cheltenham, 1987

they are currently lowest in England. Student-to-staff ratios (SSR) were approximately 7.0 in England and Scotland and more favourable in Wales.

The student/staff ratio in clinical medicine is low compared with those in other faculties in universities. The more favourable ratio of staff to students in medicine is, however, necessitated by the number (about twelve) of different clinical academic disciplines that play an essential and different role in the educational process, the need for a critical mass of staff to sustain teaching and research in a discipline, and the need to provide and supervise small-group teaching with patients on the wards and in Out-patients. Even so, extensive use must be made of NHS staff for clinical teaching that is usually organized and co-ordinated through the appropriate academic clinical department.

In undergraduate medical teaching clinical academic staff and NHS staff work in partnership with respect to the provision of both medical education and health care. Full-time clinical academic staff are involved for at least six sessions per week in the delivery of health care and form part or the whole of general or specialist firms providing acute and continuing care. This involves, as appropriate to the discipline, ward work, out-patients, endoscopy, work in operating theatres, and medical diagnostic services. They participate fully in on-call emergency rotas with NHS staff, and within teaching health districts academic clinical units provide up to 25 per cent of health care in their discipline to the local population, as well as specialist care for patients referred from more distant parts.

The contribution to clinical services by academic units is matched on the NHS side by the involvement of virtually all senior medical and many junior medical hospital staff as well as ancillary medical staff in undergraduate medical education. Indeed, the majority of the on-ward and out-patient experience of medical students is supervised by NHS medical staff because of the necessity for small-group teaching and the fact that the NHS staff usually outnumber clinical academic staff by some five to one. With respect to primary health care, student experience of general practice usually includes working for up to one month in a one-to-one ratio with a general practitioner; this necessitates the employment by universities as part-time teachers of substantial numbers of general-practitioner principals.

The importance of NHS input into medical education makes it appropriate to consider local financial provision for health care

Table 6.6 Health expenditure 1985–6 on hospitals and
community health and family practitioners services, *per capita*

	Health and community health	Family practitioners
England	225.4	69.2
Wales	240.4	70.9
Scotland	286.3	71.8

Source: *Hospitals and Health Services Year Book,* 1987; Central Statistics
Office, *Annual Abstract of Statistics,* London, 1987

from the DHSS, the Welsh Office, and Scottish Home and Health Departments as well as the provision of the Department of Education and Science when considering medical education.

Health expenditure estimates and provisions are conveniently summarized in *The Hospitals and Health Services Year Book.* The 1987 edition indicates provisional expenditure on the hospital and community services and family practitioner services 1985–6; using the population figures for England (46,463,000), Scotland (5,131,000) and Wales (2,792,000) of the 1981 census [21] the *per capita* expenditure can be calculated (Table 6.6).

This indicates a marked discrepancy in provision within the three countries with respect to hospital and community services. In particular it shows that in Scotland these health services are 27 per cent better funded than in England. For those who know the scene this is reflected in more generous levels of medical staffing, particularly at consultant level. The reason is historical, with the Scottish health boards associated with the medical schools in Edinburgh, Glasgow, and Tayside having derived greatest benefit, though a redistribution of resources between the health boards is in progress.

DISTRIBUTION OF FINANCIAL RESOURCES TO REGIONS AND TEACHING DISTRICTS IN ENGLAND

One of the initial tenets in the founding of the Health Service was that it should be national in the sense that the same high quality of service, but not a standardized service, should be provided in every part of the country. This principle was further stressed during the 1960s at the time when decisions were being taken with respect to the founding of new medical schools.

In 1964 the Minister of Health announced that a new medical school was to be founded in Nottingham in order to: (1) help correct the shortage of UK qualified doctors working in the National Health Service, and (2) improve health care in the East Midlands. By the early 1970s it was apparent that the Nottingham conurbation, which had a catchment population of 650,000, was 100 consultants short of the average district general hospital level for England and Wales and in major disciplines shared one senior registrar with equivalent disciplines in Sheffield.[22] Similar deficiencies existed in all hospital specialties and in general practice. Fortunately, this deficiency was recognized by the UGC during the early years of the school and the period of earmarked allocations of money for medical education to the university. Thus for a time some of the deficiencies in NHS consultant staff could be made good by the establishment of clinical academic posts in appropriate disciplines.

During the late 1960s and early '70s attempts were made by government to equalize the distribution of money for health care across the country, replacing a historic justification with one based primarily on population and need. After various abortive attempts the Resource Allocation Working Party (RAWP) was appointed in 1975 with the following terms of reference:

To review the arrangements for distributing NHS capital and revenue to RHAs, AHAs and Districts respectively with a view to establishing a means of securing, as soon as practicable, a pattern of distribution responsive objectively, equitably and efficiently to relative need and to make recommendations.

Its report, *Sharing Resources for Health in England*, was published in 1976 [23] and the recommendations were adopted.

RAWP in action

The target revenue allocation for each authority was based on the needs of the estimated population, weighted to reflect different use of facilities, local morbidity, and standardized mortality ratios

Table 6.7 Progress of regional health authorities (RHAs) towards RAWP revenue targets and relative *per capita* expenditure

Region	Proportion of Revenue Target Provided 1977–78	1982–83	1987–88	Expenditure* cash limit per capital 1986–87
N.E. Thames	115.8	112.8	109.0	255
N.W. Thames	117.5	110.6	105.7	217
S.E. Thames	114.2	109.3	102.7	233
S.W. Thames	106.6	106.2	100.3	215
Mersey	96.4	99.5	100.1	223
Wessex	94.0	94.6	99.3	187
South Western	95.3	95.7	99.0	205
Oxford	107.2	98.2	98.2	171
North Western	90.2	94.6	97.9	228
Northern	90.9	95.1	97.9	216
Yorkshire	95.8	96.4	97.8	206
West Midland	94.2	96.1	97.8	201
Trent	90.9	94.5	96.8	195
East Anglian	94.8	94.5	96.2	192

* Calculated from population estimates (Health and Personal Social Services Statistics for England 1986, and The Hospitals and Health Services Year Book 1987).

(SMR) as well as age and sex. The appropriateness of some of these markers has been questioned, especially that of condition-specific SMRs, and the system is currently under review.

Calculations were made for each of the fourteen English regions, the target for each being the level that would reflect equity. In 1977/8 nine regions were below target and five above (Table 6.7). The difference between the worst and best funded regions was 27.3 per cent. Within regions marked variations also occurred between districts, with some being only some 80 per cent of target. This situation applied particularly in Trent, which embraces urban populations, many of which are supported by heavy engineering and mining, as well as scattered rural populations.

Since 1977/8 yearly adjustments have been made to national regional allocations, creating RAWP-losing and RAWP-gaining

Figure 6.1 Relative funding levels of the English regional health authorities, 1986–7. Based on Trent Regional Authority publication *Achieving a Balance* (1987)

Percentage of RAWP target

regions (Table 6.7). At the local level a regional RAWP was introduced with the aim of achieving a similar equalization of provision between areas and/or districts. In Scotland a similar system of resource equalization between the health boards has been introduced – the Scottish Health Authorities Revenue Equalization (SHARE).

In consequence of the application of RAWP previously deprived regions and populations have experienced a marked improvement in the standard of health care from a poor initial baseline, while the RAWP-losing regions have experienced an uncomfortable reduction of finance that has necessitated major economies. In

Figure 6.2 Progress of district health authorities in Trent towards RAWP targets, 1982–7. Based on Trent Regional Health Authority publication *Achieving a Balance* (1987)

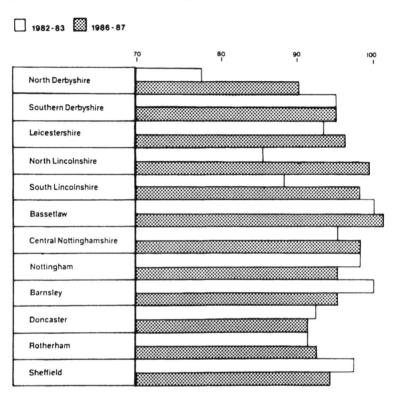

1987/8 the gap between the worst and best funded regions narrowed to 12.8 per cent (Table 6.7, Fig. 6.1), with five regions receiving greater than RAWP target funding and nine less. The best funded is currently at 109 per cent RAWP target and the worst at 96.2 per cent. The move towards more uniform funding within a region is illustrated for Trent (Fig. 6.2), in which Leicester, Nottingham, and Sheffield are teaching districts.

SIFT

In spite of the move to equalization of funding, it is apparent that there is still a gross discrepancy *per capita* (Table 6.7). Furthermore it was realized from the outset that the money being redistributed was inadequate to meet the needs of the teaching districts with medical and dental schools. RAWP therefore sought to devise a means of supporting and protecting the additional service costs incurred by the NHS in providing clinical teaching facilities for individuals who would, in the majority of cases, make a career in the NHS. The allocation is geared to the number of clinical students working in the various regions and was, and is, referred to as 'a service increment for teaching' (SIFT). Similar support is provided in Scotland, Wales, and Northern Ireland.

The problems inherent in determining relevant parameters and philosophies for the calculation of SIFT have been discussed by Bevan.[24] As observed by Bevan the 1987 rate was £27,000 per clinical medical student, and clinical dental students were funded at approximately one-third of this level. With the need to provide facilities for the teaching of over 1,000 clinical medical students in North East Thames and Trent (one of the worst funded regions) but with over 230 in all regions, the SIFT allocation has been vital for the maintenance of both teaching and health care during the period since 1981 when serious staff losses have occurred within universities. During this period of staff losses university medical faculties have usually suffered to a greater extent than others by virtue of the greater turnover in junior academic clinical staff, who hold academic posts for only limited periods as part of their postgraduate medical training programme, the majority eventually obtaining consultant posts in the NHS. The situation was also greatly aggravated by the underfunding of clinical academic pay awards and inflationary rises in prices.

It has been calculated [25] that during the period 1981–4 medical schools in England and Wales and their university hospitals lost the equivalent of the academic support and staff of two medical schools, with a partial recovery in 1984–7. The losses of university-funded staff that had serious consequences for health care were often made good by appropriate appointments funded by the NHS, sometimes categorized as 'consultants with special responsibility for teaching'.

As indicated above, when in 1964 the Minister of Health announced that a new medical school was to be founded in Nottingham, one of the reasons given for its location was to improve health care in the East Midlands. Since that time the Southampton and Leicester medical schools have been founded and it can be said, without fear of contradiction, that in all cases vast improvements in health care have followed, benefiting not only the local but also surrounding districts, and in a number of cases the academic units have made significant contributions on the national scale.

CONTRIBUTION OF MEDICAL SCHOOLS TO NHS TRAINING AND EDUCATION

Apart from some polar weighting, with a historical concentration in Scotland and London, medical schools in Great Britain are now reasonably equally distributed throughout the country. All function as centres of excellence in health care as well as national contributors to medical education at both undergraduate and postgraduate levels.

The importance of basic medical science and clinical academic units in postgraduate training for higher degrees and specialist diplomas is often overlooked and undervalued, since, in general, neither activity results in academic credit or financial gain to departments from university funds. Although the NHS is willing to pay, at sessional rate, NHS and university-funded staff for contributions to postgraduate teaching, this in no way ensures the adequacy of staffing within individual medical school departments, which are funded only with respect to undergraduate degree-course students and registered postgraduate students taking higher degrees (MSc, MPhil, PhD), i.e. degrees other than those traditionally taken by medical postgraduates: doctorates of medicine and surgery. If, as is hoped, the SIFT allocation is upgraded to meet more realistically the extra costs of teaching regions and districts due note should be taken of staffing needs of academic departments to meet NHS postgraduate training programmes that can be adequately provided only in medical schools and teaching hospitals. An alternative solution will be for the DHSS and UGC or its successor the University Funding Council to accept the need for the provision of education for medical postgraduates and essential ancillary workers, including nurses, physiotherapists, radiographers, and occupational therapists, etc., and fund them accordingly. It is worth recording that in order to meet local medical needs, and as a contribution to the knock-for-knock arrangement between the universities and the NHS, many departments of anatomy or human morphology are contributing between 200 and 300 hours teaching a year, without the provision of extra staff and inevitably to the detriment of research output.

With the intake of medical undergraduates to universities controlled by government and geared to the needs of the NHS, the UK operates what is probably the most effective system in the world of vocational professional medical training and education. Not only does limiting the intake of students to national professional need virtually eliminate the possibility of real medical unemployment, it also reduces to a minimum the extra provision and cost of health care occasioned by undergraduate teaching.

Since the medical undergraduate curriculum involves participation in clinical practice and leads on directly to pre-registration house officer appointments (the number of these available nationally is geared to the anticipated number of medical graduates per year), it is essential that both practical and theoretical sides of the educational programme should be adequate and relevant to the demands of patient care as well as serving as a basis for continuing postgraduate education and practice. Hence staff involved in vocational training in university medical schools have a greater responsibility in the professional sense than those involved in non-vocational university courses. Teaching commitments command respect, expertise, and a significant amount of time but are currently ignored as a performance indicator, to the great disadvantage of medical science and clinical departments which carry heavy teaching loads relating not only to medical undergraduates but also to postgraduates and medical ancillary workers.

In view of the heavy demands of teaching and activities relating to the provision of health care, it is of particular interest to note that, from UGC statistics [26] with respect to the most easily measured performance indicator, 'Specific expenditure, research grants, contracts and others', clinical medicine outperforms any other university cost centre when specific expenditure is compared with total costs met from general income. Thus in 1985–6 for Great Britain specific expenditure (derived research grants, etc.) was 126 per cent of the expenditure from general income from public funds, this level being boosted somewhat by the inclusion of the medical postgraduate institutes with the returns from London University.

However, when the London returns are separated, university clinical medicine other than London shows a specific expenditure of 96 per cent general income, while London returns 176 per cent, the difference being due mainly to the external (non-UGC) funding of the postgraduate institutes.

Non-UGC income generated by clinical academic departments includes grants awarded mainly by the Medical Research Council, the Wellcome Foundation, medical charities, the DHSS, health authorities and industry (mainly pharmaceutical). Clinical academic departments together with NHS colleges play a major part in hospital ethical committee-approved drug evaluation studies with respect to the products of the pharmaceutical industry.

Medical science departments also do well in obtaining grant support for research projects, though access to industrial funds is usually less readily obtained than in the case of clinical departments, except for departments of pharmacology. A true evaluation of research funds generated by FTE staff committed to medical education and employed in basic medical science departments only is impossible as a result of the current UGC cost centre classification.

Finance raised from grants or from contract work is clearly a useful performance indicator of activity. It is, however, important to note that no direct relationship exists between the amount raised and the long-term value of the research output. Furthermore, the amount that can be raised and consumed per year varies greatly between different departments (both medical science and clinical) according to (1) the nature of the research, morphological research being vastly more time-consuming than many procedures (to the disadvantage of those involved in structural biomedical research and particularly in departments of anatomy and pathology); (2) their necessary involvement in teaching (university under-graduates, postgraduate students, and NHS postgraduate medical and ancillary workers) and in the provision of health care; (3) the extent to which staff serve on the many faculty, university, and health service committees and on national councils, committees, and inquiries. Thus the current use of externally funded research work as the main performance indication of academic excellence is resulting in an increasing reluctance on the part of staff to engage in other activities, at both local and national levels, since participation inevitably reduces the time available for research. Regrettably, from the viewpoint of medical education, this reluctance is now extending to involvement in more time-consuming aspects of teaching.

In former years, assuming a reasonable degree of managerial skill on the part of the head of department, harmony and progress (measurable in publications and national standing in teaching and research) were achieved by the best use of the talents available within the department. This harmony is currently being put in jeopardy by selectivity in funding – when and if too great a weight is put on research performance as judged by the attraction of external funds. Furthermore, the losers are not only the medical schools, already in difficulties in terms of staff recruitment owing to the financial disincentives for medical graduates of an academic career, but also medical education in general.

Medical education and research in the UK have been highly regarded internationally for many years, a fact reflected in the number of overseas undergraduates and postgraduates who spend periods in Britain each year. As organized and administered since the late 1970s it has represented a remarkable achievement in terms of common sense and compromise by individuals committed to a common goal, the improvement in health care of the individual irrespective of position of domicile in these islands. Owing to the sometimes conflicting and always overlapping commitments and responsibilities of staff funded on one hand by a university and on the other by the NHS, and the need to share accommodation and facilities, a system of 'knock for knock' (uncosted mutual assistance) has evolved that has proved to be essentially cost-effective and non-divisive. However, problems do arise regarding costing in restricted areas, particularly when unequal growth and development occur. Such problems have been met at times, or even annually, by overriding knock-for-knock and introducing realistic cross-charging. This annual cross-charging is particularly important with regard to building and ground maintenance, lighting, cleaning, audio-visual (including photographic) services, and pathology services, but would almost certainly be totally non-cost-effective and divisive for the majority of activities.

The nature and funding of the health service and education in a democracy are at least in theory determined by the will of the people as represented by those elected to Parliament. For many years, and over successive governments, Britain has spent less of its gross national product on health care in relation to both its population and its national wealth than other Western developed countries.[27] Even so, impressive growth in overall expenditure on health has occurred during the past ten years, and this has been accompanied by continued progress in health care as judged by (1) increased life expectancy from birth (1951: males 66.2 years, females 71.2; 1971: males 68.8 years, females 75.0 years; 1983: males 71.4, females 77.2), (2) the infant mortality rate (under one year) in England and Wales (1977: 14.2; 1986: 9.6), and (3) the perinatal mortality rate (1976: 17.7; 1986: 9.6).

During this period remarkable advances in diagnostic equipment and techniques and in therapy have reduced discomfort and danger for the patient and resulted in the survival, often into old age, of individuals who would in earlier years have succumbed. Regrettably, however, from the financial viewpoint, such advances have in almost all instances resulted in increased running costs. Thus the explosive developments in chemistry, physics, and the biological sciences with inevitably escalating cost implications have been paralleled by similar changes in biochemical and clinical science. The financial consequences are felt by universities on the one hand, the NHS on the other, with the medical schools and medical education – dependent on both – being caught as 'pig in the middle'.

During the 1980s attempts have been made by government to keep the percentage of GNP expended on health and on education more or less constant. In order to do so it has been assumed that, in any body funded primarily from public funds, correcting inefficiency within the organization would allow targets to be met without extra financial outlay. The consequence has been the commissioning of individuals and bodies to make re-commendations on methods of improving managerial efficiency in the health service (Griffiths) and universities (Jarratt and Croham, the discussion document of the Advisory Board for Research Councils, *A Strategy for the Science Base*, and the Oxburgh Report on strengthening university earth sciences.[28] All these are currently having or are likely to have profound effects on the structure, organization, management, and function of both partners involved in medical education.

One fundamental difficulty in the quest for efficiency is that, unlike manufacturing or retail industry, increased throughput in the NHS inevitably generates at least a proportional increase in cost once the work force is working effectively. Beyond a certain point, e.g. in the time taken to clean and remake beds, even such statistics as relate to bed occupancy will show a reduction as cleaning time approaches case stay time. Anecdotal stories retailed in ignorance of true facts or with an 'economy of truth' can all too often result in witchhunts which are totally counter-productive to the main aims and achievements of the body concerned.

In Britain over the past fifty years in both the health service and the universities an effective system of administration and delivery has evolved by trial and error which has been remarkably effective in terms of cost and productivity, and which has resulted in both health services and a system of higher education that are greatly respected world-wide and are often used for postgraduate experience and training. Within the universities, given the constraints imposed by democratic ideals in terms of management, the pyramidal departmental structure has usually resulted in efficient management of what were always limited financial resources. In the health service, in the absence of a hierarchical senior medical staff structure, more difficulties have arisen, or potentially exist, and much has depended on goodwill, work ethos (usually remarkably high), a moral commitment to the system and an often genuine, if undeclared, respect for senior staff who, in the light of experience, hopefully can see the best and most cost-effective way ahead. So far as the NHS is concerned, national policy and local practice have been greatly influenced by input from professional bodies, including the British Medical Association and the royal colleges.

There is no doubt that financial cut-backs relating to costs and salaries during the past six years have resulted in some rationalization of services and better use of, or sales of, buildings. However, the use of highly selective performance indicators that relate to only a fraction of the activities that are demanded of staff in both NHS and universities makes it difficult to evaluate the effects of the introduction of the new breed of managers and management stucture. Currently within the NHS in many parts of the country the best managers were formerly the best administrators, but owing to relatively poor recruitment and rapid movement as reorganization is superimposed on reorganization, there is a major weakness in middle management. Furthermore the need for clinical audit and a degree of clinical management (by clinicians) becomes ever more evident. Within the universities the ability of departmental heads and other senior staff to administer, manage, teach, and research effectively is being eroded by the hours spent on an ever proliferating number of committees. So that the activity of, and hence existence of, departments of national and international standing are being threatened in the quest for public accountability and efficiency.

For twenty years prior to 1980, in spite of cost limits applied to universities and to the hospital and community health services, the established medical schools had survived and the new schools evolved and, indeed, shown increased productivity in terms of student numbers and research output (as is evident from university annual reports). A major factor in this development, which was inevitably dependent on adequate funding, was the fact that when the funding derived from one side (NHS or university) was reduced, as a consequence of government policy and action, the other was either maintained or fractionally increased in real terms. For the first time, and due largely to the failure of DHSS and DES to meet pay awards in full over the whole range of staff employed, and to meet the cost of inflationary rises in prices, the funding of medical schools and teaching hospitals is now being reduced by simultaneous cuts (in real terms) in DES and DHSS finance. In the opinion of the majority of those with no political axe to grind who work within the systems little or no further significant efficiency savings are possible, and already there is good evidence that shifting resources is now usually robbing Peter to pay Paul and destabilizing or making functionally ineffective the donor sector.

The difficulty in determining appropriate cost-effective policies within the NHS is only too well illustrated by decisions made over the past fifteen years with respect to the provision of community hospitals and services and the size and specialist content of district general hospitals.

Given the acceptance of the unavoidable need for cost limits, it is essential that national priorities are established in the light of current and future needs and not as a subsidiary to an economy exercise. They should relate to national needs with respect to specific activities, e.g. medicine and medical education, rather than being a broad sweep across all disciplines and professions. They must take full account of the need for fundamental and applied research and for health care in an ever-changing scene which is unlikely to be less costly, for intrinsic reasons and by virtue of public expectations. With morale now at an all-time low in the universities and the health service alike, it is essential that the reappraisal begins immediately and that those involved fully understand the working realities and complexities of the organizations and disciplines.

NOTES

1. F.N.L. Poynter, *The Evolution of Medical Education in Britain*, London, 1966.

2. Royal Commission on Medical Education, 1965–8, *Report*, London, 1968 (the Todd Report).

3. Poynter, op. cit., n.1.

4. *Centenary of the General Medical Council, 1858–1958*, London, 1958.

5. ibid.

6. General Medical Council, London, February 1980.

7. Medical Act, 1956, section 10(1).

8. Courtney Dainton, *The Story of England's Hospitals*, London, 1961; J.E. Pater, *The Making of the National Health Service*, London, 1981.

9. *Report of the Committee to Consider the Future Numbers of Medical Practitioners and the Appropriate Intake of Medical Students*, London, 1957 (the Willink Report).

10. *Report of the Medical School Advisory Committee*, University of Nottingham, June 1965.

11. Royal Commission on the National Health Service, *Report*, London, 1979; Department of Health and Social Security, *Patients First: Consultative Paper on the Structure of Management of the National Health Service in England and Wales*, London, 1979.

12. *Report of the Interdepartmental Committee on Medical Schools*, London, 1944 (the Goodenough Report).

13. Willink Report, op. cit., n.9.

14. Todd Report, op. cit., n.2.

15. ibid.

16. Department of Health and Social Security, *Hospital Medical Staffing: Achieving a Balance*, London, 1986.

17. Todd Report, op. cit., n.2.

18. K.R. Hill, 'Cost of undergraduate medical education in Britain', *British Medical Journal*, I (1964), 300–2.

19. University Grants Committee, *University Statistics, 1985–86*, III, *Finance*, Cheltenham, 1981.

20. ibid.

21. Central Statistical Office, *Annual Abstract of Statistics*, London, 1987, Persons present.

22. J.R.A. Mitchell, 'The unkindest cut of all: a view of the UGC cuts from Britain's first twentieth-century medical school', *Lancet*, II (1982), 540–5.

23. Resource Allocation Working Party, *Sharing Resources for Health in England*, London, 1976 (the RAWP Report).

24. G. Bevan, 'Financing the additional service costs of teaching English medical students by the Service Increment for Teaching (SIFT): an exposition and critique', in *Financial Accountability and Management*, ed. G. Bevan, Oxford, 1987, 147–60.

25. University Hospitals Association and National Association of Health Authorities in England and Wales, *A Survey of Academic Medical Staffing Changes in the Clinical Medical Schools and (University) Clinical Faculties in England and Wales, 1981–84*, London, 1985; B.J. Harries, J.D.M. Richards, and P. Richards, 'Academic medical staff changes in England and Wales, 1984–87', *Lancet*, II (1987), 746.

26. University Grants Committee, op. cit., n. 18.

27. Office of Health Economics, *Health Expenditure in the United Kingdom*, London, 1986.

28. DHSS circular DA(83)38, *NHS Management Enquiry* (the Griffiths Report), 25 October 1983; *Report of the Steering Committee for Efficiency Studies in Universities* (the Jarratt Report), London, 1985; *Review of the University Grants Committee* (the Croham Report), Cm. 81, London, 1987; Advisory Board for Research Councils, *A Strategy for the Science Base*, London, 1987; *Strengthening University Earth Sciences: Report of the Earth Sciences Review* (The Oxburgh Report), London, 1987.

FURTHER READING

F. Dainton, *Reflections on the Universities and the National Health Service*, Oxford, 1983.

Office of Health Economics, *Understanding the NHS in the 1980s*, London, 1984.

ACKNOWLEDGEMENT

The author is greatly indebted to Mr K. Punt (Regional Treasurer, Trent Region) and Dr M. Beavers (Department of Community Medicine and Epidemiology, University of Nottingham) for the provision of some of the Health Service data.

7

Science

Sir Alan Cook

INTRODUCTION

The relations between the economy and university science are complex and many. On the one hand, there will not be universities unless an economy produces sufficient surplus to sustain scholars, and science, which is nowadays often very expensive, takes a great deal of surplus production. On the other hand, almost all the surplus now produced in the most effective economies depends upon that rational understanding of the natural world which is science and upon there being sufficient people educated to a high level in the ways of science and engineering. The balance between those and other aspects of the relations between science and the economy is not easy to strike and within the poorer economies is probably impossible – most countries in the 'Third World' are unable to generate within themselves the knowledge and education that are needed to raise their economies. There are also great difficulties for university science in industrialized countries, such as many in Western Europe, although here the problem is perhaps less of actual resource than of dismissive attitudes to learning and scholarship. Generally, indeed, it seems to be recent experience that a satisfactory balance between the resources to be put into university science and the gains (not by any means directly economic) to be had from it can be attained only on a larger scale than the present nation State.

Modern economies depend upon the sciences, and most societies of today expect to support universities, but science is not pursued only in universities, and universities do many other things than science. This chapter is about the way in which the science done in universities interacts with the economy; in particular, it is about the way it does so in this country, for that is different from what happens in many other societies, such as some of our neighbours in the EEC. The distinctive feature in Britain is that research and teaching go on in the same department, often, usually, by the same people. There are very good reasons for that, although it seems it is difficult for administrators and others out of touch with day-to-day teaching and research to appreciate it. Teaching at the university level must be informed by current research, and research is often stimulated by teaching. Specious arguments may be advanced about separating undergraduate teaching and research, which are obviously not applicable to postgraduate teaching, yet increasingly the boundaries between the methods of undergraduate and postgraduate teaching in the sciences are being blurred, and the need in undergraduate teaching for experience of research is, if anything, growing. None the less, in many other countries much research is conducted in institutes like those of CNRS in France, or the Max Planck institutes in Germany, or in federal laboratories managed by, but not part of, US universities. The British arrangement is somewhat unusual and means that the cost of universities includes a greater component for scientific research than elsewhere, and that the direct economic benefit to the community is a great deal more than the education of professional scientists. Indeed, the purely industrial return from research seems to dominate much of the assessment of the value of university science at present.

The range of science is very great and some parts, because of particular professional associations, have very special features. In consequence I say nothing of medical science (see chapter 6), and almost nothing of agricultural or veterinary science. My discussion covers the sciences which are generally taught in most universities and which are supported through the Science and Engineering Research Council and the Natural Environmental Research Council. They have in common that research is not constrained by professional requirements and that quotas are not set nationally for admissions to undergraduate courses.

Before going on to a discussion of the present situation in education and research, something must be said of the historical development of an economy based on science and of the place of science in the universities of this country.

HISTORY

The aim of the scientist is to give a rational account of the world around, to see the world not as an incoherent assembly of unrelated facts, but as having an organization and logical structure, and to elucidate and understand it. [1] That desire to understand in a rational way has been a dominant feature of mankind from the early Greek natural philosophers onwards; it is at once part of the human condition and helps us to comprehend the human condition. It is natural philosophy, but it goes beyond philosophy as understanding because of the predictive power of understanding nature, which enables nature to be changed by the works of art that are engineering. Thus it has direct economic consequences. That was always so, but the major changes in societies, from agricultural to industrial bases, came about in Europe only with the development of heat engines and the associated sciences of mechanics and thermodynamics in the second half of the eighteenth century. Although the sciences were pursued in the universities by people who, like Newton or Halley, were also men of affairs or, like Hales or Ray, were medical men, the developments that led to industrialization did not, for the most part, come about in universities. Black was a university professor, but Watt, Joule, and Carnot were not, and the experimental sciences were not taught to undergraduates at that time. Industrialization was further carried forward by electrical power and communications, at the hands of such as Faraday, Kelvin, Maxwell, and Hertz, with university associations somewhat more significant, but no one at that time would have thought it important that universities should pursue science for industrial purposes. By the 1870s, however, the lack of good scientific education in the universities of Britain was causing concern and Maxwell established an undergraduate experimental laboratory as an essential part of physics teaching at Cambridge. Increasingly, since then, the relevance of university science to industrial progress has been emphasized, until now it seems to some the only justification for scientific studies, or indeed for universities at all. We do indeed depend for our present manner of life upon a great range of highly successful scientific research – electric power, electronics, organic chemistry of many sorts, nuclear physics, pharmacology, physiology, and others beside. The connection between economic return and the aim of the research on which it depends is, however, often very far from direct. When J.J. Thompson undertook the work which led him to discover the electron, he did not do so in order to make television sets, or any of the other devices which depend on electrons for their operation. He wanted to understand nature; even if television had occurred to him as a desirable aim, he could not have known that to produce it he had to discover the electron, because until he discovered the electron he did not know that the electron existed or that it had the properties that fitted it for use in television. We can make small or moderate steps in technology by choosing research on the basis of what we already know; the revolutionary changes come from discovering something we do not already know.[2] Thus although our present economies arise from the science of the past and are sustained by the science of the present, there are few direct connections in detail between the science done in our universities and the effectiveness of the economy.

INDUSTRIAL APPLICATIONS

It is the industrial applications in science in universities that seem always to be in question when university science is discussed. Certainly scientific discoveries in universities have had, and do have, many applications in industry, in medicine and in other parts of the economy. Many antibiotics, notably penicillin, were discovered and to some extent developed in university laboratories. Much chemical research in university departments is done with the support of industry or in the knowledge of the needs of industry. Many of the principles employed in solid-state devices in the electronics industries were established in university research in departments of physics. For all that many applications have flowed from scientific research in university, industrial applications are subsidiary to other reasons for pursuing science in universities. First, university departments cannot compare in scale or drive or equipment with a major commercial laboratory, given a clear objective. The outstanding example is the development of the transistor, undertaken because the policy-makers of the Bell Telephone System realized that the heat generated in thermionic valves set severe limits on long-distance telephone systems.The Bell Laboratories could put far more money, far more equipment into seeking a solid-state device than any university department of physics or engineering, and they succeeded. Likewise, firms such as IBM, or Hughes Aircraft, or Xerox, or ICI, or Burroughs Wellcome, if they identify a profitable product, can devote far more to developing it than possible in any university. When it comes to major developments based on understood principles, university activities can only be subsidiary. Of course, there is often room for commercial exploitation of some imaginative piece of university work, and that is the basis of science parks in the vicinity of universities, but the firms that result are commonly specialized and small, as from the Cambridge Instrument Company onwards, and while they may make a good living for their owners, they do not in general make much of a difference to the gross domestic product.

Those who work in universities are often castigated because, it is said, their discoveries are brilliant but the development and application are poor. But not everyone is or should be an industrialist. It is the entrepreneurs of industry who are supposed to have the imagination to see markets and the drive to develop them; if British use of British discoveries is poor, it is the entrepreneurs and industrialists who have fallen down on their own job and it is somewhat unreasonable to blame university people for failing to do the industrialists' job for them, in such time as they may have to spare from teaching and research.

The great effect of university research on industry has been and is still, for the most part, at arm's length, and it has been and is of outstanding importance, especially when, as in recent decades, it has been in parallel or in partnership with that in public or industrial laboratories.

University research has made great contributions to industry generally, rather than to particular individual applications, in a whole range of modern technology – aircraft and aero-engines from their inception until now, electronics, opto-electronics, engineering materials, engineering processes, structures, computers, control systems, pharmaceuticals, fertilizers, dyes, petrochemicals. None the less, such developments could, like the transistor, or much of radar or nuclear energy, equally well have come about in industrial or government laboratories. The direct economic return from university research is not great; to my mind it is not possible that it should be great. The importance of university science to industry is elsewhere, in teaching and in the advancement of the general rational understanding of nature and man.

THE UNDERSTANDING OF THE NATURAL WORLD

Human society and activity of almost all sorts and almost everywhere depend upon scientific discoveries and ideas that have for the most part emerged quite recently. We can scarcely eat without scientific agriculture, travel without aerodynamics or the internal combustion engine fitted with micro-computers, listen to or observe works of art without electronics, all these dependent on great power at our disposal, to keep us comfortable, to drive our machines, to execute great programmes of civil engineering, power which comes from nuclear fission or oil, sources deriving from very recent scientific developments. When we fall sick or suffer accidents, from causes which increasingly arise from our life based on science in so far as the bacteriological infections of the childhood of most of us have been overcome by modern pharmacology, then we depend for diagnosis or cure or correction or alleviation on physical devices or chemical drugs that have become available from industrial or university research only quite recently.

We well know that life is longer, easier, fuller, more human for most people in many societies as a consequence of living in an economy based on the sciences, but we also know that the economy brings with it great dangers. How do we balance benefit against risk, who is to make the choice? In this country we elect or appoint politicians to do it for us. Unfortunately it is very evident that neither the electors nor those who appoint, neither the elected nor the appointed, are sufficiently aware of the scientific facts and principles upon which depend the decisions to be taken. With very few exceptions, even the journals of quality devote little space to science and technology, and that only when something judged sensational happens. These matters cannot be dismissed as issues restricted to economics; there are political and moral considerations which are at least as important as the economic, and each depends on the other – a moral position without economic means or political will may be condemned as frivolous, just as an economic decision taken against moral principles is wicked. None the less, to make proper decisions, one must know what may be the consequences of some act in the real world around us, or, if that cannot be known, then one must assess the extent and consequences of ignorance.

In many matters of public concern it is not that very subtle issues are involved. Rather is it that it is difficult for people (including many undergraduate students of science) to grasp quite elementary matters that are far from common experience. To illustrate this point I comment on three issues where it seems to me that ignorance of principles is widespread, and I think that what is common to them, and indeed to the layman's appreciation of science generally, is not so much ignorance of fact but lack of understanding of the sort of argument the scientist employs in trying to attain a rational understanding of nature.

My first instance concerns decisions on the balance between coal and nuclear power. Some matters are clear-cut – the technical matters of materials for high temperatures, or machines for automatic mining, which of the two sources produces electricity more cheaply, taking all costs into proper account, the effect of the balance on the political power of the National Union of Mineworkers or the Electricians' Union, but the discussion of safety seems often shrouded in emotion. Yet the facts seem straightforward matters of statistics, and it may be curious (or is it?) that a society so given to the study of chance at horse racing or the pools should have difficulty in appreciating statistical arguments. One fact is that those directly involved in nuclear power generation have a negligible risk, per megawatt hour of power generated, of death, accident, or sickness, as compared with those directly involved in coal mining and power generation from coal.

The indirect risks, to those not directly employed, are less readily quantified, and are perhaps worth further study, but risks from getting cancer if you live near a nuclear power station seem almost certainly less than those of pollution from coal (or oil) fired power stations.

The risks of power generation are straightforward to estimate, for they are stable over long periods of time, with one exception – the risk of the single very exceptional accident. The theory and practice of statistics and probability are very inadequate for treating the rare event. Rare events do, however, have great importance, economically, morally, and politically, especially when they are natural events that we have no means of controlling but only of anticipating and ameliorating. Large earthquakes in California, or New Zealand, or even Japan, are rare. How much resource should be put into provision against them, to the detriment of other, on-going, activities? Should earthquake warnings be given, if they depend on imperfect understanding of the origin of earthquakes, and if the consequences of crowds flocking out of San Francisco or Los Angeles may be worse than those of the earthquake itself? Here again is a great complex of economic, political, and moral questions made very difficult to address by reason of our poor understanding of the physics of earthquakes and statistics of rare events. Fortunately in Britain we do not have to deal with such matters directly, but analogous ones do have some relevance for us, economically, morally, and politically, in that they arise in assessing what sort of help we should be giving to countries in the Third World. A rather obvious, but apparently little considered, fact about such countries is that they are situated in regions of hostile climate, with considerable chance of major disaster from typhoons, tidal waves, droughts, and so on, and in regions also of great seismic and volcanic risk. Simply giving money seems beside the point when it is very difficult to use money in effective ways because there are very few indigenous skilled technologists, engineers and administrators, but great distances and difficulties of communication.

Common to the instances I have adduced is a lack of appreciation in most discussion of the magnitudes of physical quantities. As an island people we are sadly unaware of the magnitudes of quantities related to the seas, so that we have poor appreciation of how difficult the oceans are to control and of the constraints they impose on our activities, for instance in seeking to use the tides or waves as a source of power.

The issues, and others like them, that I have raised here are economic and they are scientific; they ought to be matters of study and teaching in universities. It is not difficult to argue that in their economic and political implication they are at least as significant as the direct industrial applications of university science.

EDUCATION

An economy founded on science requires men and women well educated in the sciences for it to work. The technical activities of industry depend on the direct practice of science and on administrators with a deep, up-to-date understanding of science. Many of the failures of British industry may be ascribed to poor understanding of the facts and methods of science among those who determine policy. Beyond industry itself, the whole functioning of an economy dependent on science requires administrators, politicians, and electors who have a reasonable scientific understanding of the world around us, its physical opportunities and constraints. The economic efficiency of modern society is dependent on a high level of scientific education. The universities alone have education as their principal end. No one else can do it.

Scientific education in universities has a number of purposes. Many university teachers, being also deeply involved in advancing knowledge, see their principal and most rewarding aim as bringing on successors in research, and the scheme of university undergraduate courses, consciously or unconsciously, looks forward to the MSc or PhD degrees. Teaching to the high level needed to train research workers is indeed essential to educate those who are going to follow professional careers in industry, but many undergraduates will have careers in which scientific understanding is needed without engaging in professional or original work. They need to understand what is going on in the world around them without themselves contributing to it scientifically. Of course, teachers in schools are by far the most important, and, as is only too well known, it is very difficult to attract sufficient good students of science into school teaching.

Just as there is considerable, unjustified emphasis on the immediate industrial applications of university research, so there is unjustified emphasis on training for machines and processes now in use. That is unrealistic and short-sighted. In ten – in five years, indeed – after graduation the university graduate may well find himself confronted with problems hardly foreseen in his courses, so rapid is technical change. Universities must above all educate their students to think scientifically and originally, rather than train them to today's techniques, out of date tomorrow. With that goes the need for continuing education. The university teacher, because of his teaching and research, of necessity keeps abreast of new work and applications – if he is any good, some of them are his – but the students he taught ten years before are slipping behind. How may they be revived? In an economy based not just on science but on rapid change in science and its applications, education goes on for ever. The universities, and those who provide funds for them and their students, have hardly moved in the matter.

English university undergraduate courses are for three years. Those who graduate with a degree in science are supposed to be able to embark on a professional scientific career, albeit in a subordinate way, or to begin a training in original research. That scheme is plainly unrealistic nowadays. The bulk of fact goes beyond what students should be asked to assimilate and organize in three years, particularly when standards of essential subjects like mathematics are falling in schools, and apparatus that the graduate will encounter in his employment is far beyond the resources of most university science departments, not only for undergraduate teaching, but for much postgraduate training as well. The great increase in computer facilities and possibilities, especially their use in undergraduate teaching, exacerbates the situation. If British universities are to educate the scientists the economy needs just to keep going, let alone those needed to understand and spread understanding, the breakdown of the three-year undergraduate courses must be recognized and the resources given for four-year courses and up-to-date equipment. Clearly that is very expensive.

THE COST OF UNIVERSITY SCIENCE

It would be unrealistic to write about the place of university science in the economy without considering its cost. There is a dilemma. To sustain and advance the economy, more and better scientists are needed, remembering that in this country the proportion educated at universities is less than in almost any other country with a comparable economy, and that scientific research in universities is also beginning to compare unfavourably in scope and achievement with that elsewhere. Yet to meet all those needs would require funds three or four times as large as at present on a conservative estimate, together with additional sums to bring scientific equipment up to date. The dilemma is not one that will go away with changed politics, for the cost per student of universities and of the scientific work done in them can only increase absolutely.

A solution to the cost of research may be sought in pooling resources between groups of universities, not just in this country but within Europe and internationally. That has developed rather spontaneously in high-energy physics in particular, where experiments at CERN are run in collaboration by groups from universities in different countries. As the cost of scientific research increases – as it is bound to, for the deeper one probes into nature, so the more elaborate, more powerful equipment one needs; as the cost increases, so must university groups increasingly pool their resources, and science be thought of as European or world-wide. It is natural for some sciences to develop in that way, especially the geophysical sciences, which take the whole Earth as their object, but expense is driving others. When the groups from different universities are working together it is natural to ask whether there should not be a closer association of universities themselves, whether we should not be getting ideas from the medieval university, where, as now, there were common economic problems, a common culture, and a common recognition of teachers and scholars.

CONCLUSIONS

The economies of industrialized societies depend on the scientific understanding of the natural world, upon a goodly number of highly trained and educated scientists, engineers, and administrators, and upon the continual development of new applications of scientific knowledge.

The universities' contributions are principally to education in the sciences, but historically they have contributed more extensively and at the deepest levels, as well as developing some applications in lesser ways.

Sensible and acceptable decisions in our economies require a scientific approach and an awareness of scientific considerations among policy-makers and the population generally. That is plainly lacking, especially in the Treasury.[3]

Rational thought and understanding are above all what set human beings apart from beasts. It is perverse to see the purpose of thought and understanding as solely economic advancement; rather a main aim of economic activity should be to further understanding. The denigration of knowledge for its own sake in the name of industrial efficiency is intellectual treason.

NOTES

1. See the evidence of the Royal Society to the House of Lords Select Committee on Science and Technology, *First Report*, London, 1986, para. 2.2.

2. Other examples are the work of Faraday on electromagnetism (the basis of electrical power generation and transmission), the discovery of the atomic nucleus and nuclear transformations by Lord Rutherford and of the neutron by Chadwick, the investigation of penicillin and the elucidation of the structure of DNA and the molecular basis of genetics.

3. For an opinion of the Treasury see the view of the Select Committee of the House of Lords, op.cit., n.1, para. 6.30: 'it remains disturbing that a department as powerful as the British Treasury has, in effect, and as a consequence of its particular evolution, a definite blind spot in science and technology.'

Conclusion

Michael D. Stephens

My bank manager speaks of universities as a luxury. In such attitudes are encapsulated the reasons for the relative economic decline of Britain over the last century or so. Those societies much quoted as paragons of economic virtue are notable for high investment in all types of education over a long period. Within that generous allocation of the nation's resources, higher education is rarely neglected. Even the Department of Education and Science's doubtful and complacent document *International Statistical Comparisons in Higher Education* (1987) revealed that of each hundred persons of the 18–24 age group, the United Kingdom had fifteen in higher education whilst France had nineteen, West Germany twenty, Italy eighteen, Japan twenty-one, the Netherlands twenty-two, and the United States forty-four. To take the latter, the same document showed that the United States puts 2.5 per cent of its gross national product into public expenditure on higher education, as against the United Kingdom's 1.1 per cent. On the assumption that we should judge ourselves against the best, then the United States is our yardstick.

America has a belief in the importance of education which is not to be found among the English population as a whole. To use Massachusetts briefly as a case study, as it was the pacemaker in American industrialization, it is notable that sixteen years after the first successful European settlement (in 1620), Harvard was established. Although it is famed today as a private university, initially·it gained much of its funding from the State's allocation of revenues, such as that from the Boston-to-Cambridge ferry across the Charles River. The first State-supported free school in Boston was available by 1635. By 1841 the taxpayers of Massachusetts, with its population of 700,000 were putting £130,000 into educational provision whilst the British government was spending £30,000 on the education of England's 15 million population. As Massachusetts achieved near universal literacy in the seventeenth century Americans came to assume that education should be available for everyone. The belief and the reality have not always matched up, but it can surprise nobody that America is the place where a citizen has the best chance of access to a university. The English belief that university places should be available for only a small percentage of the population contrasts baldly with the United States' philosophy. We have neither the *per capita* quantity of university places nor an institution the equal of Harvard. My bank manager's belief that a university education is only a consumer good suggests that America has been unwise in the allocation of its national resources over the last three and a half centuries. How curious that its economy is so much more productive and creative than ours.

Robert Taylor, the Labour editor of *The Observer* newspaper, wrote a carefully researched article (12 June 1987) under the title 'The thick man of Europe'. He stated, 'Our badly educated labour force, from management downwards, remains one of the primary causes of our post-war economic decline as our competitors adapted far better to technological change and we lost the protected markets of our former Empire'.

Although Taylor's focus was clearly indicated with his opening statement – 'Britain has the worst industrial training system of any sizeable economy in the Western world. This was a tragic truism over 100 years ago at the height of the first Industrial Revolution and it is still so today' – the relevance of university education is not missed. Apparently only 21 per cent of British managers have a degree or professional qualification of any kind. Such a state of affairs would be unthinkable in Japan.

When Charles Handy lectured at the Royal Society of Arts on 23 February 1987 his theme was 'The future of work – the new agenda'. In terms of the role of universities what is so significant for the future is the quotation:

McKinseys in the Netherlands estimate that 70 per cent of them (the 24 million jobs in Britain) will be cerebral jobs, knowledge jobs that is, information jobs, not manual jobs: a complete switch from one hundred years ago when over 70 per cent of all jobs were manual. Remember that manufacturing will by 1990 be employing only 21 per cent of the workforce and that if that manufacturing is going to be of any value, then most of that 21 per cent will be doing clever jobs. The days of the factory hand are gone for ever.

What is so remarkable about all those looking at present statistical trends and then forecasting the future in societies such as Britain is their universal agreement that the work force will need to be well educated, as manual jobs are fast disappearing. Nobody predicts a growing demand in any developed country's economy for physical labour. At a time when the British government recognizes the need for the whole population to have a good grounding in the three Rs, more forward-thinking states have moved far beyond that. The whole population will need to be highly educated in a broad-based way to have the confidence to move easily in a rapidly changing world. As America is already showing, a flexible definition of what is a graduate, supplemented by a relatively high percentage of the population with doctoral degrees, gives huge economic advantages over the British approach of very low national priority given to higher education. As Handy warns:

> No one will survive, let alone succeed, in the new world of work who cannot communicate and work with others, who cannot think for himself or herself, who cannot demonstrate some competence, some saleable skill if you like, and who cannot push and shove and take initiatives. Of course the best of British have always done these sort of things, but the best was 10 per cent or perhaps 20 per cent. I'm talking about a minimum of 70 per cent.

The Americans have recognized such new realities in practical terms, with an easy acceptance in key states, like Massachusetts or California, of a graduate equivalent of 50 per cent of the population. They will find it possible to aim for that 70 per cent-plus mentioned by Handy being 'graduates'. Britain's government finds it virtually impossible to accept such views. We still have a belief that the rule-of-thumb men who created the industrial revolution are the answer to economic success in the late twentieth century. We continue, as did our misguided Victorian forebears, to seek working men and women of 'natural genius'. There is much talk of 'entrepreneurs'. Such ideas were already dangerously out of date in the 1830s when key countries like Prussia and Saxony were demonstrating that the economies of the second stage of the industrial revolution would be based on science and technology with a highly educated leadership.

These themes are much in evidence in the contributions to this book. Whilst the previous chapters could not be accused of self-satisfaction and complacency, they do indicate the substantial gap between governmental thinking and that of opinion leaders within universities themselves. As Professor Martin warns, 'We need to be very wary of those who, perhaps in positions of political power over education, tell us what is and will be useful'. Or as Professor Sir Alan Cook states, '... the problem is perhaps less of actual resource than of dismissive attitudes to learning and scholarship'.

There seems to be a destructive tension between those who believe that universities are a simple vehicle for producing graduates tailored to specific economic needs and those, often equally simple in their aspirations, who talk of the universities as places of self-fulfilment. What takes place in a university is, and should be, complex. It should serve both individual needs and the demands of the economy. To quote Professor Taylor on the key area of education:

> there is no evidence that the vast majority of university school of education, college and polytechnic staff are unaware of the importance of a soundly-based and successful economy if the political freedom, social harmony and qualities of aesthetic response that they value are to be maintained.

Dr Shinn reminds us that:

> A modern complex industrial society has vocational and manpower needs. A sophisticated system of higher education developed within a liberal environment committed to freedom of expression also has needs if it is to fulfil successfully the objectives to which it is dedicated in its charters. The arguments for the rights of the university are interesting, if somewhat academic, in a period of economic growth. These same arguments are critical in a period of recession and consequent reduction in public spending.

Governments are fond of justifying their actions by mentioning the mandate of the people, even when, as is the case in Britain, only a minority of the electorate has voted for them. This has been used to override contrary obligations such as university charters. For example, the 1884 charter of University College, Cardiff, seems to have been of little value in protecting that institution when it committed the cardinal sin within a monetarist world and overspent. Amalgamation with the University of Wales Institute of Science and Technology was the price of waywardness. Such ruthlessness by a government which can write off £900 million on an unsuccessful airborne radar system at about the same time would seem ironic and demonstrates very effectively Whitehall's seemingly lower priority for State-funded education, as against defence. As Professor Sims argues, government:

> must get over the naïve compulsion that it seems to have acquired under a monetarist philosophy of always expecting that someone else will readily accept that it is their responsibility to do it and not that of the government itself.

In April 1987 the government published *Higher Education: Meeting the Challenge*. Whilst there is much to commend the government's views on the future of higher education (presented to Parliament in April 1987) the previously stated traditional limitations are present. These include the long-standing belief that higher education is 'expensive', and a desire to focus it more narrowly. These are repeats of our nineteenth-century weaknesses. Critics at the beginning of that century were fond of pointing out that only Turkey had as few universities as England. Having managed to broaden out the universities' curriculum in the nineteenth century from their obsession with classics, we are now to narrow it again, with, probably, engineering as the lauded priority area.

In the opening 'Aims and purposes' section of the paper it is stated that 'Higher education should: serve the economy more effectively; pursue basic scientific research and scholarship in the arts and humanities; have closer links with industry and commerce, and promote enterprise'. These admirable, but limited, objectives seem to freeze out many other purposes, despite the statement that the government accepts the Robbins Committee's definition of higher education, 'instruction in skills, the promotion of the general powers of the mind, the advancement of learning, and the transmission of a common culture and common standards of citizenship'. Throughout the document such narrowness is stressed; for example, in the 'Access' section it is stated that 'To take greater account of the country's needs for highly qualified manpower the

Government will: plan for student numbers to increase in the next few years, to return to present levels in the mid-1990s and then to grow again; study the needs of the economy so as to achieve the right number and balance of graduates in the 1990s'. As the government has been unable to get the number of primary-school places right when it knows the number of live births, the latter point should cause higher education disarray by the next century.

The crunch statement is 'The Government and its central funding agencies will do all they can to encourage and reward approaches by higher education institutions which bring them closer to the world of business'. Whilst this abandons the broader-based objectives of less mechanistic higher education systems such as that of the United States and Japan, it does have some limited spin-off for areas like recurrent education. The 'Access' section continues:

[The government will] plan to increase participation rates among young people, particularly young women, and mature entrants – by building on improvements in schools and colleges, and in admission arrangements for those with non-traditional qualifications; further develop continuing education, particularly professional updating.

It is a pity that continuing education is seen in such very limited terms, and the text seems only interested in the much quoted PICKUP initiative model. Harold Wiltshire's great vision of an education system which produces 'reflective citizens' is an alien one to present government thinking.

The document often ignores its own good sense. Besides recognizing the importance of increasing mature student entry to higher education, and developing further at least some forms of continuing education, it also states, 'It is hard to forecast the long-term demand for specific skills'. This is at variance with innumerable proclaimed objectives such as that of 'more selectively funded research, targeted with attention to prospects for commercial exploitation'. Economically more successful countries have larger higher education systems which do not attempt to predict future needs. They favour broad-based initial higher education, followed by specialization, and, above all else, an ability to see lifelong education as the only effective way of meeting changing economic and social education needs.

Higher Education: Meeting the Challenge is, of course, a

political document. It reflects the policies of the present government, and has to demonstrate that the first two terms of 'Thatcherism' had been a success. This is done both honestly and dishonestly. To take an example of the latter, it is claimed:

> The best like-for-like comparison is probably of the proportion of the relevant age groups gaining degrees and higher diplomas. On that basis Britain is on a par with attainments in France and ahead of the rest of the European Community, though achievements here are not as good as those in Japan and the USA.

This means, say, that the Dutch, who often go to university for a seven-year full-time programme, are to be seen as comparable to the British, who do a one- or two-year diploma. A more honest yardstick would be numbers coming from higher education with doctoral qualifications, or at least masters' and doctoral degrees.

We have a demoralized higher education system. Whilst many of the government's ambitions for it are admirable, the approach has been heavy-handed and the vision too narrowly focused. There are anti-intellectual traditions in Britain which underpin our relative economic decline. We are a long way from the lifelong education system needed by our country. There lies one of the substantial parts of the economic contribution of universities in the future: new and established knowledge and ideas made easily available to citizens throughout their lives. As always, the universities will do it well, but be less appreciated for their excellence than if they were players in the money markets.

Index